pressure cooking
for everyone

pressure cooking
for everyone

RICK RODGERS AND **ARLENE WARD**

PHOTOGRAPHS BY **KATHRYN RUSSELL**

CHRONICLE BOOKS

SAN FRANCISCO

Library of Congress Cataloging-in-Publication
Data available.

ISBN 0-8118-2525-6

Printed in Hong Kong.

Prop stylist: Kathy Longinaker
Food stylist: Dierdra B. Bugli
Assistant food stylist: Barbara Bugli
Design: Elizabeth Van Itallie

Distributed in Canada by Raincoast Books
9050 Shaughnessy Street
Vancouver, British Columbia V6P 6E5

10 9 8 7 6 5 4 3 2 1

Chronicle Books LLC
85 Second Street
San Francisco, California 94105

www.chroniclebooks.com

acknowledgments

Rick would like to thank:

Diane Kniss for her constant support as a friend in and out of the kitchen.

Kelly Volpe for her invaluable help as kitchen assistant and general hand-holder.

T-Fal for supplying pressure cookers for testing, as well as interesting conversation on the joys of pressure cooking.

Arlene Ward for showing me a new way to cook.

Patrick Fisher for his valued comments as house food critic and incomparable skill as head pot-washer.

Arlene would like to thank:

Dean, for being such a great husband—it's not easy being married to a cook.

Ruedi Keller for the opportunity to work with Kuhn-Rikon pressure cookers over the years.

All of the students in my pressure cooking classes at Adventures in Cooking for proving to me that there are a lot of people who love pressure cookers.

Rick and Arlene would like to thank:

Bill LeBlond for wanting to turn his appreciation of pressure-cooked cuisine into a cookbook.

Stephanie Rosenbaum, who skillfully guided the book through different stages of publication.

Lisa Wolff, our copy editor, for her gentle but thorough work on the manuscript.

Kathryn Russell, photographer; Diedra B. Bugli, food stylist; Elizabeth Van Itallie, designer; and Julia Flagg, Chronicle Books designer, for making our recipes look so good on paper.

table of contents

beans

risotto and grains

quick pasta sauces

vegetables

desserts and fruits

rick rodgers introduction

As a traveling cooking teacher, I see a lot of different cooking schools. They are always busy places, and the staff and I never seem to get to sit down to eat something before we start an evening class. (It's not a good idea to teach a cooking class on an empty stomach.) However, I noticed that at one particular school, the owner, Arlene Ward, always managed to find the time to make dinner.

One night we sat down to a delicious meal of perfectly cooked lamb chops in an herbed mustard sauce. This meal had been cooked while I left the room for ten minutes! It was like magic. When I asked Arlene her secret, the answer was short and to the point:

"I made it in the pressure cooker."

I had never eaten anything that had been cooked in a pressure cooker. Either you grew up in a house that had one, or you didn't. Frankly, I didn't, and I just never got around to learning about them. I had written a book on crockery slow-cookers, and I thought that was the only appliance for cooking stews, ragouts, and the like. What had I been missing?

Over the meal, Arlene and I discussed how she used the pressure cooker almost every night to make dinner for her husband and herself. And she made another whopping remark, in almost conspiratorial tones:

"I make all of the stock for the classes in the cooker, too. It takes about one-third of the time, and everybody loves it."

If cooking teachers are particular about anything, it is the stock they use in classes. We know that a good stock makes good food. And if some of the best chefs in America have been using Arlene's pressure-cooked stock at her school, that proved to me that my head had been in the sand too long.

Arlene shared some of her recipes with me, and I learned the basics of pressure cooking from them. We agree that the pressure cooker really shines when used to reduce the cooking time of dishes with prohibitively long preparations, such as soups, stocks, stews, ragouts, beans, long-cooking vegetables, and pasta sauces. But I was also delighted to find that in addition, it can be put into action to create some surprisingly excellent versions of dishes you would never expect to take out of a cooker, such as flan, cheesecakes, and meat chops.

That's when this cookbook was born. We have collected the recipes we love to cook and the food our families love to eat. You'll find family favorites that will have the kids asking for seconds, as well as more sophisticated fare that is fit for company. We are not such enthusiastic fans of the pressure cooker that we want to convince you that it does *everything* well. In our opinion, it's not worth learning to cook pasta and regular rice in a pressure cooker just to shave a few minutes off the cooking time. We have included lots of tips, hints, and frank observations to ensure that you have success every time you use your pressure cooker.

Arlene has been a fan of pressure cooking for years. She began by using the old-fashioned pressure cookers to make dinner for her family. (The old models are the ones that people used to joke about because someone they knew misused one and exploded split pea soup all over the kitchen.) I came onto the pressure-cooking scene after the pots had been redesigned and improved with new fail-proof safety features. Believe me, these new pressure cookers are no joke! They are beautiful, sleek, and efficient additions to anyone's kitchen. In our kitchens, the term "letting off steam" is a good thing, because it means that a great-tasting meal will be on the table in minutes!

A few years ago, at a kitchenware buyers' show, I noticed display after display of pressure cookers. While I had been cooking with one for years, these were pressure cookers with a difference. First of all, instead of the utilitarian, workhorse design of my old aluminum cooker, they were beautiful appliances that looked like they came out of an elegant European kitchen. The high-end machines were made of gleaming stainless steel with thick bottoms to discourage any scorching of food. The jiggle-top valve on the old models had been replaced by a variety of more efficient and easy-to-control devices. Live demonstrations of the cookers showed that the hiss of escaping steam from the old clunkers had been greatly reduced and often eliminated.

The salespeople did not have to convince me of the pressure cooker's ability to make great food—I had a husband and two grown children who had been enjoying my pressure-cooked meals for quite some time, and they had been very well fed. When Mom is a food stylist and cooking teacher, the family expects good food, and the pressure cooker never disappointed. The revival of pressure cooking made sense. Everyone these days is busy, and unfor-

tunately, when time is shaved from some people's schedules, the kitchen is the first place to suffer. We want good food, but we just don't have the time to cook it. After a tough day at work, wouldn't it be nice to be able to make a comforting stew or a pot of long-simmered pasta sauce without having to cook for hours? The pressure cooker can make dinner for you in a fraction of the time.

Even though my old cooker had design problems, I was forgiving. However, I began carrying the new pressure cookers in my kitchenware shop. And I started teaching pressure-cooking classes to see what new converts I could make.

Both experiments were unqualified successes. The promise of tasty, quick food from a pressure cooker attracted a number of curious cooks. After my classes, students didn't just leave with full stomachs, they left with pressure cookers, too. Many times, it wasn't long before they returned to buy another, smaller cooker so they could prepare a main dish and a side dish at the same time. Or, they would return a third time to buy a cooker as a gift because they wanted to share their "discovery" with their friends. I have to smile at people who treat pressure cooking as something new, although I will admit that the new cookers certainly take much of the old guesswork out of the technique. Before long, I got a call from my pressure-cooker supplier telling me that my shop had generated the most sales of their appliance in the country!

I have cooked many wonderful meals in my pressure cooker, but as with any appliance, it is important to know its strengths and avoid its weaknesses. Rick and I have cooked many different things in the cooker over the years, and we feel it's important to guide you towards the dishes that the cooker does best, rather than make empty promises. Because we're both cooking teachers, we believe that good cooking goes beyond just following a recipe, and is based on an understanding of techniques. When you understand how something works, you can apply that knowledge every time you cook. So we'll start out with a thorough explanation of the mechanics of pressure cooking, then move on from there to recipes for hearty stews, light chicken and fish dishes, a selection of our favorite bean, grain, and vegetable dishes, pasta sauces, and even desserts.

If you're new to pressure cooking, we hope to show you the ropes. And if you're an old hand like me, we have a few surprises up our sleeves. There's something in this book for everyone.

letting off steam: pressure cooker basics

To acquaint yourself with your pressure cooker, read the instruction manual well. The manufacturer is best equipped to explain each model's details. Here are the most common questions about pressure cooking.

How does a pressure cooker work?

At sea level (where the atmospheric pressure is 14.7 pounds per square inch [psi]), water boils at 212°F. Even if the pot is covered, as steam gathers from the boiling liquid, it will escape and keep the temperature steady. With a pressure cooker, the lid is locked onto the pot, and a rubber gasket ensures that the steam is trapped in the pot. As it has nowhere to go, pressure builds up in the pot, and the temperature rises above 212°F. If allowed to build to high pressure, the temperature will reach 250°F, or 38°F above the standard boiling temperature, and the pressure in the pot will be 15 pounds psi above the atmospheric pressure outside the pot. Some pressure cookers can be adjusted to cook at medium (235°F and plus 10 pounds psi) and low pressure (220°F and plus 5 pounds psi). *Most of the recipes in this book are cooked at high pressure.* Safety valves in the lids of the cookers release the steam to maintain a safe level of pressure. The steam and pressure must be released before the lid can be opened.

How does pressure cooking reduce cooking times?

Because of the higher temperature, increased pressure, and steam, the food cooks much more quickly than usual. The three factors combine to soften food fibers in tough meat and vegetables in record time and to heighten flavors.

What are the health benefits of pressure cooking?

In the open pot used in conventional cooking, vitamins and minerals can be lost in the steam and cooking liquid. Because pressure cooking is a "closed" system and the food cooks in shortened periods of time, more nutrients are retained. In addition, vegetables keep their natural colors better because they are not exposed to oxygen. Healthful low-fat, high-protein dried beans and legumes can be pressure-cooked in a fraction of their traditional cooking time, making them much easier to add to the diet.

What are the different types of pressure cookers?

Jiggle-top or weight-valve. This is the old type of pressure cooker, but there are still inexpensive models available. They are usually made from aluminum, which is a great heat conductor, but it can give a metallic taste to dishes that use acidic foods like tomatoes and wine. This type of cooker has a heavy, removable weight that fits on top of the steam-vent pipe in the center of the lid. After the pressure builds and the steam is released through the vent, the steam "jiggles" the weight. Some models come with different weights that allow the food to be cooked at different pressure levels.

Stationary pressure regulator. Most new models have pressure regulators built into their lids. Some have spring-operated rods that rise to indicate the pressure as it builds in the cooker. Some have dials that can be adjusted to set the pressure level, and others have both dials and rods. These machines are quiet and efficient. They are usually made from heavy-gauge stainless steel with a thick mixed-metal bottom to conduct heat and discourage scorching.

What size pot is the most versatile?

The 6-quart pot is the industry standard. (Note that some European models use liters to indicate the capacity of the pot. As a liter isn't that much bigger than a quart, consider them interchangeable.) We tested the recipes in a 6-quart pot, but most of them will work in 5- to 7-quart models. A wide selection of pressure cookers is available in sizes from 2½ to 12 quarts. The smaller, skillet-shaped models are perfect for cooking chops or dinners for two, and serious cooks love the large-capacity pots that can make quarts of stock at a time. Buy the cooker that fits into your lifestyle. Or, look for sets that have a couple of cooker bottoms with interchangeable tops. You may find yourself wanting two sizes for cooking flexibility. (Don't confuse large pressure cookers with pressure-cooker canners, which are designed specifically for processing jars of food.)

If you are buying your first pressure cooker and trying to decide between models, take your own height into consideration. Some tall pots are difficult for shorter cooks to see into. (Arlene has taken to standing on a box when this happens; Rick is not height-challenged.)

What are the new safety features in today's pressure cookers?

Many design changes have occurred over the years to improve the reliability of pressure cookers. First, the lid must be locked in place in order for the pressure to rise. After the food is cooked, you will not be able to open the lid unless the pressure has been completely released. Overpressure and/or backup plugs have been built into the cooker to relieve excess steam pressure. In spite of all of these features, it is common sense to *stay in the kitchen while using the pressure cooker.*

What is a good way to familiarize myself with my cooker?

The following procedure not only allows you to get to know your cooker's fine points without using groceries, it also removes any factory odors before actually cooking. Wash the cooker well, inside and out, with hot soapy water. Remove and wash the rubber gasket, and replace it in the lid. Fill the pot with 2 cups of water. Lock the lid in place and bring to a boil over high heat. Adjust the heat to maintain the pressure, according to the manufacturer's instructions. This usually means that a very fine stream of steam is released through the regulator, and a gentle hissing is heard (some models are silent).

Note the burner heat level needed to maintain high pressure. If you have a difficult time finding a proper heat level (usually the burner heat is too high and causes an excess of pressure buildup), use a heat diffuser under the pot. Heat diffusers are especially useful when using pressure cookers on electric stoves. To be sure you have found the right level, cook the water for 10 minutes. Remove the pot from the heat and release the pressure. Don't be surprised if the cooker makes a fair amount of loud hissing!

If your cooker has low pressure, fill it with another 2 cups of water and cook the water for 10 minutes at low pressure to familiarize yourself with that level, too.

What kinds of food are best in the pressure cooker?

When you want to quickly prepare foods with traditionally long cooking periods (meat stews and ragouts, pasta sauces, soups, stock, dried beans, grains, and firm vegetables), the pressure cooker will become your best friend in the kitchen. The steamy cooking interior also creates an ideal atmos-

family favorites

Here are some recipes in the book that we turn to again and again for everyday meals. We've found that kids like many of these dishes, too.

Quick Chicken Soup

Minestrone

Green Pea Soup with Ham

Turkey and Root Vegetable Soup

Abilene Beef and Bean Chili

Old-Fashioned Beef Stew with Carrots and Potatoes

Italian Pot Roast

Yankee Pot Roast

Corned Beef Boiled Dinner

Sweet-and-Spicy BBQ Country Ribs

BBQ Chicken

Hunter's-Style Chicken

Mexican Chicken in Soft Tacos

New Orleans Red Beans and Rice

Wheat Berries with Carrots and Currants

Spanish Rice with Sausage

Brown Rice Pilaf with Peas

Summer Tomato and Basil Sauce

Three-Meat Bolognese Sauce

Spaghetti and Meatballs

Jalapeño and Cheese Corn Pudding

Steamed Potatoes with Dill Butter

Quick Garlic Mashed Potatoes

Creamy Rice Pudding

Cranberry Bread Pudding

Chocolate Pots de Crème

"No-Cook" Orchard Applesauce

phere for making creamy custards and cheesecakes and many fruit desserts. With a couple of minor alterations, fish and poultry dishes can be prepared successfully in the cooker, too. We feel that most foods with delicate textures and relatively short cooking times are best prepared with traditional cooking methods.

Most manufacturers warn against cooking certain foods because they sputter, foam, or froth, and can block the pressure release valve or steam vent. These include split peas, pasta, rhubarb, and oatmeal. Beans tend to foam, too, but a tablespoon of oil drizzled over the cooking liquid keeps the foaming down. Applesauce and cranberries are two other possible "bad guys," but we have found ways to make them usable in pressure cookers (see "No-Cook" Orchard Applesauce on page 159 and Pear-Cranberry Chutney on page 164).

What are some of your tips for pressure cooking?

We give specific tips for different types of food at the beginning of their respective chapters. Here are some general rules for pressure cooking.

• *Never fill the cooker more than two-thirds full,* or the boiling food may clog the vent and block safe escape of the steam. When cooking foods that swell, such as beans and grains, do not fill the cooker more than half full. Remember, a half-full 6-quart cooker is still 3 quarts, and that is a good amount of food.

• *Wipe the rim of the pot clean of any spills before attaching the lid,* as the food could break the seal and prevent pressure from building.

• *Clean the vent area well after each use to remove any food.* If the vent is clogged, the pressure may build to dangerous levels. If you have a jiggler-type cooker, clean the vent pipe with a wooden toothpick to be sure it is clear. If you have a spring-valve cooker, press the rod to be sure it moves freely.

• *Check the condition of the rubber gasket often.* The rubber gasket plays an important role in the pressure cooker. Replace any gasket that is dry, cracked, or damaged in any way. (In an emergency, you can try to prolong the life of your gasket by wiping it with vegetable oil, which may temporarily seal any cracks.) The gasket should be replaced every year, or sooner if necessary. It is a good idea to have a spare gasket on hand. Refer to your manufacturer's manual for the phone number for replacement gaskets.

• *Always use a kitchen timer when pressure-cooking food.* A digital timer works best, especially when timing short cooking periods in seconds. Exact timing is often very important. Set the timer for the cooking time while the pot is building pressure. When the proper level is reached, start the timer. This way you won't miscalculate the cooking time while you set the timer—sometimes the few seconds taken up while fumbling with the timer makes the difference between food that is overcooked or perfectly cooked.

How much liquid do I need to cook with to maintain pressure?

The pressure cooker needs liquid in the pot to build up the steam and pressure that cooks the food. This amount varies with each model. Check the manual to see the minimum amount for your cooker. If it doesn't state the amount, add ½ cup water to the pot and attempt to bring it up to pressure over high heat. If it doesn't come to pressure, release any steam in the pot, add another ¼ cup water, and try again. The amount of water used to reach pressure is the minimum amount of required liquid. Wet ingredients like crushed tomatoes and moist ingredients that give off juices or liquid (such as onions) count as liquid.

If your cooker requires more liquid than the recipe calls for, add more broth or water as needed. The finished cooking liquid will be thinner, and will need to be boiled down longer or thickened with additional cornstarch or flour.

Many of the recipes in this book call for homemade stock or canned broth. We make homemade stock often in our pressure cooker, and store it in the freezer, ready to defrost when needed. However, you can certainly use a high-quality, low-sodium canned broth, if you wish. (Low-sodium broth will not oversalt the final dish, and, in our opinion, just tastes better than regular broth.) One can of broth is about 14 ounces, just shy of 2 cups. Instead of opening up another can to make up the 2-ounce difference, just dilute the broth with a little water.

What are some cooking terms specific to pressure cooking?

• *Cook for 20 minutes at high pressure.* Pressure cooking has very different cooking times than traditional methods. At the end of each recipe, we specify the cooking time and the amount of pressure so you have a better idea of what to expect. We don't include the timing for auxiliary steps, such as browning the meat or thickening the sauce.

• *Place the trivet and steamer basket in the cooker.* Most of the recipes in this book are cooked directly in the pot in a flavorful liquid. However, some vegetables and desserts are cooked by steam alone, and should be raised above the water level with a trivet and steaming basket. If your cooker did not come with these two items, use a collapsible aluminum steamer basket for vegetables. For desserts that need a flat surface, place an empty tuna can, opened at both ends, in the pot, and top with a flat plate that allows a ½-inch space between it and the sides of the pot.

• *Lock the lid in place.* Attach the lid according to the manufacturer's instructions. If the lid is not attached properly, steam will not build. Be sure the gasket is in place and undamaged.

• *Bring to high pressure over high heat.* Most of the recipes in this book are cooked at high pressure. To bring the pressure up as quickly as possible, turn the burner to high. If you have a gas stove, do not let the flames lick up the sides of the cooker. Don't forget to use this period to set the kitchen timer.

• *Adjust the heat to maintain the pressure.* When you have reached high pressure according to your model's specifications, first turn on the kitchen timer to start timing the food. Immediately reduce

company fare

When company's coming, the pressure cooker can help you get an elegant meal on the table in record time without any compromises in flavor or quality. The following are dishes that we have served to company with great success.

Borscht with Beef Shanks and Fresh Beets

Provençal Onion Soup

Deviled Short Ribs

Beef Brisket with Onion-Raisin Sauce

Cuban Pot Roast with Capers and Olives

Five-Spice Pork Roast

Pork Chops with Cherry–Black Currant Sauce

Lamb and White Bean Ragout

Rolled Butterflied Leg of Lamb

Loin Lamb Chops Dijonnaise

Veal Roast with Prosciutto, Sage, and Lemon

Osso Bucco Presto

Chicken with Tarragon-Mustard Sauce

Turkey Breast with Marsala and Mushrooms

North Beach Cioppino

Normandy Fish Chowder with Saffron

Tuna Steaks in Basque Sweet Pepper Ragout

Pinto Bean Salad with Chile Vinaigrette

Risotto with Porcini and Parmesan

Risotto with Butternut Squash and Sausage

Shrimp and Saffron Risotto

Holiday Wild Rice with Dried Cranberries

Pasta with Wild Mushroom Sauce

Artichokes with Minted Vegetable Broth

Potato Salad with Mustard and Herbs

Orange-Glazed Yams

Caponata

Orange and Chocolate Marble Cheesecake

Café con Leche Flan

Ginger Crème Brûlée

Riesling Pears with Mascarpone and Almonds

Pear-Cranberry Chutney

the burner heat to a level necessary to maintain the pressure, usually low to medium-low. *If anytime during cooking the cooker makes a loud hissing noise, lower the heat.* A heat diffuser may be needed to bring some burners down to the proper levels.

If you have an electric stove, the burner will take time to cool. Using pot holders, transfer the pot to a second burner, already preheated to low. Or, transfer the pot to a turned-off burner. Adjust the cooking burner to low so it can cool. After 30 to 60 seconds (the pressure in the pot should maintain for this short period of time), transfer the cooker back to the first burner.

• *Cook for 20 minutes.* While we give specific cooking times for each dish, just as with other types of cooking, the cook must be flexible. Especially with beans and tough vegetables, it is difficult to always gauge the exact cooking time to the second or minute. *Do not let this concern you!* If the meat for your stew isn't quite tender, just reattach the lid and pressure-cook the food for another few minutes. Or, if you have the time, simmer it, uncovered, until it is tender. Especially with more delicate foods, often the residual heat from the pot will continue cooking the food even after the lid has been removed. This is such an obvious rule of cooking that we don't go into detail with every recipe to inform you to cook the food further if necessary. It is better to err on the side of undercooking, then finish the cooking with one of the methods mentioned above, than to have overcooked, mushy food.

In some recipes, foods are added at different times. For example, in traditional cooking you may cook the meat with the vegetables in a stew. If they are cooked together for the same amount of time in a pressure-cooker, the vegetables might be overdone. Therefore, the meat is cooked first until almost tender; then the pressure is released, the vegetables are added, and the pot is brought back to pressure for a short period of cooking time.

• *Open the lid, tilting it away from you to block any escaping steam.* This is an obvious safety measure to protect the cook from the built-up steam.

• *Remove the pot from the heat and quick-release (or naturally release) the pressure.* There are two methods of releasing the heat, *quick-release* and *natural release*. In both cases, start by removing the pot from the heat.

The quick-release method is used for most recipes. Most modern pressure cookers have a pressure-release button or setting. Another way of releasing heat is the *cold-water technique*: Carry the pot to the sink and run cold water over the lid, taking care not to get water into the vent. The cold-water technique is very quick, but it can have an adverse effect on the food. In general, use the lid's pressure release setting and only turn to the cold-water technique as a backup in the case of a clogged vent (the releasing steam from the vent will sputter and hiss loudly).

Even though the steam released from pressure cookers is surprisingly cool, some cooks will still feel safer with some distance between their hands and the release valve of the spring-type cooker. Use a long-handled spoon to press down the valve.

When a recipe says "allow the pressure to drop naturally," no pressure-release dials are activated—the cooker is allowed to stand off the heat until the pressure is completely released through the safety valves. This takes 10 to 20 minutes, depending on the amount of liquid in the pot. Some foods with delicate textures require the natural release method because it is a gentler way to reduce the pressure and steam, and the food won't fall apart. Keep in mind that the food will continue to cook in the pot during the natural-release period.

What about cooking at high altitudes?

Because water and liquids take longer to come to a boil at altitudes above 2,500 feet, the cooking time and liquid used must be adjusted. For every 1,000 feet above 2,000 feet, increase the cooking time and liquid by 5 percent. For example, if cooking at 4,000 feet, increase the time by 10 percent (an additional 2 minutes for a 20-minute recipe), and the liquid by 10 percent (for 2 cups or 32 tablespoons of liquid, add about 3½ tablespoons).

Are there any tips for seasoning pressure-cooked foods?

Pressure cooking intensifies flavors, so about half the amount of dried herbs, spices, and salt are needed than in traditional cooking methods. Before cooking, season the food with the minimum amount of salt and pepper. After cooking, you can always increase the amount of salt and pepper to taste. Add fresh herbs just before serving—they tend to lose their flavor in the pressure cooker.

Pressure cooking also brings out the flavors in vegetables, so their initial cooking isn't as long as in other methods. For example, the onions, carrots, and celery in a traditional stew are usually cooked until well-softened and tender to activate their natural sugars. In the pressure cooker, they only need to be sautéed until barely softened, about 2 minutes.

Meats and poultry should be browned in the pressure cooker to add flavor to the cooking liquid. But do not brown them as deeply as you do with other methods of cooking—any overbrowned flavors will intensify in the pressure cooker and taste burned. The meat and poultry should be browned in batches in the pot. Do not crowd them, or they will steam and not brown.

Full-flavored oils, such as peanut or extra-virgin oils, become even more forceful when cooked in a pressure cooker. Before using them, consider whether you want their taste to permeate your dish. Sometimes, as in Tuscan Green Beans with Pancetta and Olives (page 131), the flavor is appropriate. Otherwise, a neutral, mild-flavored vegetable oil is a safer, more versatile choice.

How should I wash and store the pressure cooker?

Remove the gasket. Using mild dishwashing soap and a nonabrasive sponge, wash the gasket, cooker, and lid well with warm water. Do not use abrasive cleaners. The lid should never be immersed in water or cleaned in a dishwasher (you can put the cooker pot in the dishwasher, but it will stay shinier if hand-washed). Some manufacturers recommend cleaning the pressure regulator after each use, too.

Towel-dry the pressure cooker well before storing. Replace the gasket. Store the lid upside down on the pot. Never store the cooker with the lid locked in place. This could damage the gasket, as well as seal in cooking aromas, which will result in a bad odor when the pot is opened.

soups
and stocks

The pressure cooker is *the* ideal tool for making quick soups and stocks. It will make more than what you'll usually need for one meal, but that's a bonus. Our freezers are filled with soups and stocks in 1-pint and 1-quart containers. It's a real joy to realize that all you have to do is defrost and heat up some homemade soup and you can have a meal on the table in no time.

Soups are more than warming winter meals. Sure, they're great served piping hot when the weather is cold, but many soups are equally tasty chilled. Instead of having the stove on for hours when the sun is blazing, use the pressure cooker to create light soups in minutes. Borscht (page 29), Minestrone (page 34), and creamy Green Pea Soup with Fresh Herbs (page 39) are three classic soups

served either hot or cold. However, when chilled these soups may be better without meat and prepared with Homemade Vegetable Stock (page 26). In cold soups, the chilled fat in the meat tends to give the soup a greasy mouth-feel no matter how well it is skimmed.

A good stock is the backbone to many dishes. Canned broth is fine, but homemade stock improves any dish and is very easy to make in the pressure cooker. Low-sodium canned brands taste best and won't add excessive salt to the finished dish. Do not use bouillon cubes. They just don't taste good, and they are much too salty to use reliably in a pressure cooker, which tends to intensify the salt flavor in foods.

tips for soups and stocks

➤ At first, pressure-cooked stocks will look cloudy, because the stock has boiled in the cooker and the fat and gelatin from the bones are suspended in the liquid. You can use the stock immediately, but it improves if refrigerated before using. Allow the strained stock to cool to room temperature, then refrigerate overnight. The fat will chill and will rise to the top of the stock, where it can be scraped off with a large spoon.

➤ Stock is made from bones and used as an ingredient in a recipe. Broth is made from meat and bones, and is seasoned to be enjoyed on its own. The two are interchangeable.

➤ Never salt stock. Often the cooking liquid in a recipe is boiled down to intensify the flavors. However, the salt will remain the same regardless of the amount of liquid.

➤ The recipes in this chapter yield good-sized amounts. Plan on freezing the leftovers! Freezer-safe plastic delicatessen containers can be found at restaurant supply stores and wholesale clubs. (Or just ask your delicatessen or supermarket if they will sell you a few.) Unfortunately, not all these containers are microwave-safe. To be on the safe side, only partially defrost the soup or stock in the container. Transfer it to a microwave-safe bowl, cover, and continue defrosting.

➤ To freeze soup or stock, skim any fat from the surface. Cool to room temperature. Pour into freezer-safe containers, leaving 1 inch of head space to allow for expansion. Freeze for up to 6 months.

➤ Most of our recipes are cooked in a liquid. The fat from the meat is transferred to the liquid and should be removed. Let the cooking liquid stand off the heat for a few minutes to allow the fat to rise to the top, and use a large spoon to skim it off.

➤ Traditionally cooked stocks are always prepared with cold water. With a pressure cooker, you can use warm or hot water with no adverse effect. The warmer water brings the cooker up to pressure more quickly, and reduces the total cooking time.

homemade **chicken stock**

This is the all-purpose stock that Arlene uses for her cooking classes. Many a particular chef has complimented her on its flavor. Chicken backs, with their high proportion of bones and a modest amount of skin, make the best stock. While they are available at most supermarkets, they can be collected from cut-up chickens (see page 74) and frozen until you have enough for a batch of stock. Save and freeze the neck and giblets — except the liver — and wings, if desired, for stock, too. Chicken wings are a second choice, as the fat in the skin will make the stock cloudy at first—it definitely needs to stand for a few hours to allow the fat to rise to the top, where it can be skimmed off.

2 pounds chicken backs, all visible fat and excess
   skin removed
1 tablespoon vegetable oil
1 small onion, halved
1 small carrot, coarsely chopped
1 small celery rib with leaves, coarsely chopped
¼ teaspoon dried thyme
¼ teaspoon black peppercorns
4 parsley sprigs
1 bay leaf
2 quarts water

1. Using a heavy cleaver, chop the chicken backs into 2- to 3-inch pieces. (You may ask the butcher to do this.)

2. In a 5- to 7-quart pressure cooker, heat the oil over medium-high heat. In batches, add the chicken and cook, turning occasionally, until lightly browned, about 5 minutes. Transfer to a plate and set aside.

3. Pour all but 1 tablespoon of the fat from the pot. Add the onion, carrot, and celery. Cook, stirring occasionally, until the vegetables soften, about 2 minutes. Return the chicken to the pot. Stir in the thyme, peppercorns, parsley, and bay leaf. Add the water.

4. Lock the lid in place. Bring to high pressure over high heat. Adjust the heat to maintain the pressure. Cook for 40 minutes.

5. Remove from the heat and release the pressure naturally. This will take about 20 minutes. (You can also quick-release the steam, but the natural-release cooks the stock a bit more to extract additional flavor.) Open the lid, tilting it away from you to block any escaping steam. Strain the stock into a large bowl. Cool completely. Cover and refrigerate overnight.

6. Using a large spoon, remove the chilled fat from the surface of the stock. (The stock can be prepared up to 3 days ahead, stored in an airtight container and refrigerated, or frozen for up to 6 months.)

———————

Makes about 2 quarts
40 minutes at high pressure

homemade beef stock

While we have been known to use a can of chicken broth, canned beef broth isn't as reliable. Before we became pressure-cooker fans, making homemade beef stock was admittedly a chore rather than a pleasure. Now, whenever we see beef bones at a good price at the market, it's a cinch to whip up a batch. Plainly put, the flavor of homemade stock is incomparable to canned stock, and it is especially important in recipes where the flavor of the stock isn't masked by other ingredients, such as Provençal Onion Soup (page 37).

1 tablespoon vegetable oil
2 pounds beef bones, sawed by the butcher into
   1- to 2-inch-thick pieces
1 pound cross-cut meaty beef shanks
1 small onion, coarsely chopped
1 small carrot, coarsely chopped
1 small celery rib with leaves, coarsely chopped
1 garlic clove, crushed
1 tablespoon tomato paste
¼ teaspoon dried thyme
¼ teaspoon whole black peppercorns
4 sprigs fresh parsley
1 bay leaf
2 quarts water

1. In a 5- to 7-quart pressure cooker, heat the oil over medium-high heat. In batches, add bones and shanks and cook, turning occasionally, until lightly browned, about 6 minutes. Transfer to a plate and set aside.

2. Pour all but 1 tablespoon of the fat from the pot. Add the onion, carrot, celery, and garlic. Cook, stirring occasionally, until the vegetables begin to soften, about 2 minutes. Return the bones and shanks to the pot. Stir in the tomato paste, thyme, peppercorns, parsley, and bay leaf. Add the water. Lock the lid in place and bring to high pressure over high heat. Adjust the heat to maintain the pressure. Cook for 1 hour.

3. Remove from the heat and release the steam naturally. This will take about 20 minutes. (You can also quick-release the steam, but the natural-release cooks the stock a bit more to extract additional flavor.) Open the lid, tilting it away from you to block any escaping steam. Strain the stock into a large bowl. Cool completely. Cover and refrigerate overnight.

4. Using a large spoon, remove the chilled fat from the surface of the stock. (The stock can be prepared up to 3 days ahead, stored in an airtight container and refrigerated, or frozen for up to 6 months.)

Veal Stock: Substitute veal shanks and bones for the beef.

Makes about 2 quarts
1 hour at high pressure

homemade **fish stock**

Fish stock is one of the quickest stocks to make because the fish bones are thinner than their meat and poultry counterparts. Even so, the pressure cooker efficiently extracts the flavor from the bones in record time. As fish bones tend to foam during cooking, skim off any foam that forms while the stock comes to a boil, drizzle a little oil on top before closing the lid, and use a natural-release method to cut down on sputtering. Fish stock is delicate; if freezing, use within 2 months.

2½ pounds assorted bones, heads (no gills), and trimmings from white-fleshed fish (avoid oily varieties like salmon, bluefish, or whiting), chopped into large pieces
1 medium onion, coarsely chopped
2 medium celery ribs with leaves, coarsely chopped
6 parsley sprigs
½ cup dry white wine, such as Sauvignon Blanc
1½ quarts water, as needed
¼ teaspoon dried thyme
¼ teaspoon whole black peppercorns
1 bay leaf
2 teaspoons vegetable oil

1. In a 5- to 7-quart pressure cooker, combine the fish, onion, celery, and parsley. Add the wine. Pour in enough water to cover the fish completely, but the cooker should be no more than two-thirds full. Bring to a boil, uncovered, over high heat, skimming off any foam that rises to the surface. Add the thyme, peppercorns, and bay leaf. Drizzle the oil over the stock.

2. Lock the lid in place. Bring to high pressure over high heat. Adjust the heat to maintain the pressure. Cook for 10 minutes. Remove from the heat.

Allow the pressure to drop naturally. Open the lid, tilting it away from you to block any escaping steam. Strain the stock through a colander into a medium bowl. Cool completely. (The stock can be prepared up to 2 days ahead, stored in an airtight container and refrigerated, or frozen for up to 2 months.)

**Makes about 2 quarts
10 minutes at high pressure**

homemade **vegetable stock**

You don't have to be vegetarian to appreciate a good vegetable stock. It is another ingredient that is hard to find in an acceptable commercial version (some of them are too heavy on cabbage and beets). You'll use this stock in vegetarian dishes, of course, but try it as a substitute for meat or poultry stocks, soups, or stews. It's delicious on its own as a soup, perhaps with some pasta, rice, or beans stirred in. A good homemade vegetable stock relies on potatoes (to give the stock body) and lots of garlic (for flavor), and not on a hodge-podge of tired specimens from the vegetable cooler. Use fresh, flavorful ingredients, and don't alter the recipe so you get variable results all the time. (Would you want a beef or chicken stock that tasted different every time you made it?)

2 tablespoons oil
2 medium onions, unpeeled, cut crosswise in half
3 medium carrots, chopped
3 medium celery ribs with leaves, chopped
1 large (about 13 ounces) russet or Burbank potato, scrubbed, unpeeled, and cut into 2-inch chunks
1 head garlic, cloves crushed under a heavy knife, and peeled
2 quarts water, as needed
6 parsley sprigs
¼ teaspoon dried thyme
1 bay leaf
1 teaspoon salt
½ teaspoon whole black peppercorns

1. In a 5- to 7-quart pressure cooker, heat the oil over medium-high heat. Add the onions, carrots, celery, potato, and garlic. Cook, stirring occasionally, until the onions are golden and a light brown film forms on the bottom of the cooker, about 6 minutes.

2. Add enough water to come halfway up the sides of the cooker, about 2 quarts. Stir in the parsley, thyme, bay leaf, salt, and peppercorns.

3. Lock the lid in place. Bring to high pressure over high heat. Adjust the heat to maintain the pressure. Cook for 20 minutes. Remove from the heat and quick-release the pressure. Open the lid, tilting it away from you to block any escaping steam. Strain the stock through a colander into a medium bowl. Cool completely. (The stock can be prepared up to 3 days ahead, stored in an airtight container and refrigerated, or frozen for up to 6 months.)

Makes about 2 quarts
20 minutes at high pressure

SOUPS AND STOCKS

demi-glace **rapide**

Demi-glace is a staple in many restaurant kitchens, as chefs know that this intensely meaty essence delivers a surplus of flavor. Stir a spoonful of demi-glace into any meat sauce or gravy.

1½ pounds veal bones, with some meat attached
1½ pounds beef bones, with some meat attached
1 pound chicken backs, visible skin and fat removed, chopped into 2- to 3-inch pieces
2 cups water, plus more as needed
1 tablespoon vegetable oil
1 medium onion, chopped
1 medium carrot, chopped
1 medium celery rib with leaves, chopped
6 parsley sprigs
½ teaspoon dried thyme
½ teaspoon whole black peppercorns
1 bay leaf

1. Position a rack 6 inches from the source of heat and preheat the broiler. Spread the veal, beef, and chicken bones in a roasting pan. Broil the bones, turning occasionally, until browned on all sides, 20 to 30 minutes. Transfer the bones to a platter.

2. Pour out all of the fat in the pan. Place over two burners at high heat and heat the pan until sizzling. Pour the water into the pan and scrape up all of the browned bits in the pan. Set aside.

3. Meanwhile, in a 5- to 7-quart pressure cooker, heat the oil over medium heat. Add the onion, carrot, celery, parsley, thyme, peppercorns, and bay leaf. Cook, stirring often, until the vegetables begin to soften, about 3 minutes. Place all of the bones in the pot, being sure that they don't fill the cooker more than halfway. (If necessary, reserve some of the browned bones for the second cooking.) Pour in the liquid from the roasting pan. Add enough hot water to cover the bones by about 1 inch, but not filling the cooker more than two-thirds full.

4. Lock the lid in place. Bring to high pressure over high heat. Adjust the heat to maintain the pressure. Cook for 1½ hours. Remove from the heat and let the pressure drop naturally. Open the lid, tilting it away from you to block any escaping steam. Strain the stock through a colander into a medium bowl, saving the solids. Set the stock aside.

5. Return the bones and vegetables to the pressure cooker. (If desired, replace some of the cooked bones with the reserved browned, uncooked ones.) Add enough hot water to cover the bones by about 1 inch, but not filling the cooker more than two-thirds full. Lock the lid in place, and cook at high pressure for 1 hour. Remove from the heat and let the pressure drop naturally. Strain this stock into the reserved stock and discard the solids. Let stand for 10 minutes. Skim off any fat that rises to the surface of the stock.

6. Pour the stock into a large stockpot or Dutch oven. Bring to a boil over high heat. Boil until the liquid is dark brown, very thick, and evaporated to about 1 cup. (This can take an hour or so.) Cool completely. Transfer to a 1-cup airtight container, cover tightly, and refrigerate. (The demi-glace can be refrigerated for up to 2 weeks, or cut the chilled demi-glace into cubes, wrap each in plastic wrap, and freeze in a freezer storage bag for up to 6 months.)

Makes about 1 cup
1½ hours at high pressure, then 1 hour at high pressure

borscht with beef shanks and fresh beets

Borscht is a rib-sticking soup that is usually considered winter fare, but doesn't need to be reserved for cold weather. During the winter, the borscht with beef shanks can be served hot with chunks of tender cooked beef. But in the summer, chilled borscht (made without the beef shanks) is wonderful as a refreshing lunch or light supper. If your beets don't have any greens, don't worry—they add a touch of color and flavor to the soup, but they are entirely optional. And be flexible with the cooking time needed for the beets, as their tenderness varies from bunch to bunch.

2 tablespoons vegetable oil
1 pound cross-cut meaty beef shanks
1 medium onion, chopped
2 medium carrots, cut into ½-inch dice
2 medium celery ribs, cut into ½-inch dice
1 garlic clove, minced
5 cups water
2 cups Homemade Beef Stock (page 24) or
   canned low-sodium broth
1 cup chopped seeded plum tomatoes or one
   14½-ounce can tomatoes in juice, drained and
   chopped
½ teaspoon dried thyme
1 bay leaf
½ teaspoon salt, plus more to taste
¼ teaspoon freshly ground black pepper, plus
   more to taste
3 medium beets, preferably with greens attached
4 cups thinly sliced green cabbage (about ½ large
   head)
¼ cup red wine vinegar
2 tablespoons light brown sugar
¼ cup chopped fresh dill
Sour cream, at room temperature, for serving

1. In a 5- to 7-quart or larger pressure cooker, heat 1 tablespoon of the oil over medium-high heat. Add the beef shanks and brown on both sides, about 4 minutes. Transfer to a plate and set aside.

2. Add the remaining 1 tablespoon oil to the pot and heat over medium heat. Add the onion, carrots, celery, and garlic and cook, stirring occasionally, just until beginning to soften, about 3 minutes. Return the beef shanks and any juices on the plate to the pot. Stir in the water, stock, tomatoes, thyme, bay leaf, ½ teaspoon salt, and ¼ teaspoon pepper. Lock the lid in place. Bring to high pressure over high heat. Adjust the heat to maintain the pressure. Cook for 30 minutes. Remove from the heat and quick-release the pressure. Open the lid, tilting it away from you to block any escaping steam. Remove the beef shanks and bay leaf. Discard the bones and cut the meat into bite-sized pieces; set aside.

3. Meanwhile, cut the greens from the beets, discarding the stems. Rinse the greens well (they can be sandy) and chop coarsely. Peel the beets and cut into ½-inch dice.

4. Add the cabbage, beets and greens, vinegar, and brown sugar to the pot. Lock the lid in place and bring to high pressure over high heat. Adjust the heat to maintain the pressure. Cook for 8 minutes. Remove from the heat and quick-release the steam. Open the lid, tilting it away from you to block any escaping steam.

5. Stir the beef and dill into the soup and cook,

uncovered, to heat through, about 2 minutes. Season to taste with salt and pepper. Serve hot in individual bowls, topping each serving with a dollop of sour cream.

Chilled Borscht: Delete the beef shanks. Cook the vegetables in 2 tablespoons vegetable oil. If desired, substitute 2 cups Homemade Vegetable Stock (page 26) or canned vegetable broth for the beef stock.

———————

Makes 8 to 10 servings
30 minutes at high pressure for beef,
then 8 minutes at high pressure for beets

peasant **cabbage** and bean soup with kielbasa

Cabbage, beans, and sausage are a classic culinary trio. You'll find them served together in farmhouses from the Mediterranean to the Russian steppes, but the exact variety of smoked sausage will change from country to country. This dish uses kielbasa, showing the recipe's Eastern European provenance. If your kielbasa comes from an Eastern European butcher and has a thick casing, remove it. Supermarket kielbasa can be good, and the reduced-fat turkey variety works very well.

2 tablespoons extra-virgin olive oil

1 medium onion, chopped

1 large celery rib, sliced ¼-inch thick

1 garlic clove, minced

4 cups Homemade Chicken Stock (page 23) or canned low-sodium broth

6 cups thinly sliced green cabbage (about ½ medium head)

8 ounces kielbasa or other smoked sausage, cut lengthwise, then into ¼-inch-thick slices

One 14½-ounce can tomatoes in juice, drained and chopped

½ teaspoon dried thyme

½ teaspoon salt, plus more to taste

¼ teaspoon freshly ground black pepper, plus more to taste

1 cup dried white kidney (cannellini) beans, soaked, cooked, and drained, or one 15-ounce can white kidney beans, drained and rinsed

1. In a 5- to 7-quart pressure cooker, heat the oil over medium heat. Add the onion, celery, and garlic and cook, stirring often, until just softened, about 3 minutes. Stir in the stock, cabbage, sausage, tomatoes, thyme, ½ teaspoon salt, and ¼ teaspoon pepper. Lock the lid in place. Bring to high pressure over high heat. Adjust the heat to maintain the pressure. Cook for 5 minutes. Remove from the heat and quick-release the pressure.

2. Open the lid, tilting it away from you to block any escaping steam. Stir in the beans and cook for 1 minute to heat through. Season with additional salt and pepper. Serve hot.

Makes 8 servings
5 minutes at high pressure

quick chicken soup

Arlene devised this recipe when she had a bad cold and wanted some restorative chicken soup in a hurry. In a recent cooking contest for "Jewish penicillin" (what many New Yorkers call chicken soup because it is used to "cure" so many minor ailments), all of the well-seasoned contestants admitted that they used canned chicken broth or bouillon cubes to give their soup a boost. If it's good enough for a Jewish grandmother, it's good enough for us! If you are a white-meat person, use chicken breasts, but the thighs hold up better in the pressure cooker.

2 tablespoons vegetable oil
1½ pounds boneless, skinless chicken thighs
1 medium onion, chopped
2 medium carrots, cut into ½-inch-thick rounds
2 medium celery ribs with leaves, cut into ¼-inch-thick slices
4 cups water
2 cups canned low-sodium chicken broth
¼ teaspoon dried thyme
1 small bay leaf
½ teaspoon salt, plus more to taste
¼ teaspoon freshly ground black pepper, plus more to taste
1 cup fine egg noodles
2 tablespoons chopped fresh parsley

1. In a 5- to 7-quart pressure cooker, heat 1 tablespoon of the oil over medium heat. Add the chicken thighs and cook, turning once, until browned, about 5 minutes. Transfer the chicken to a plate and set aside.

2. Add the remaining 1 tablespoon oil to the pot and heat. Add the onion, carrots, and celery. Cook, stirring occasionally, until the vegetables are beginning to soften, about 2 minutes. Stir in the water, broth, thyme, bay leaf, ¼ teaspoon salt, and ½ teaspoon pepper, scraping up any browned bits on the bottom of the pot. Return the chicken to the pot.

3. Lock the lid in place. Bring to high pressure over high heat. Adjust the temperature to maintain the pressure. Cook for 8 minutes. Remove from the heat and quick-release the pressure. Open the lid, tilting it away from you to block any escaping steam. Transfer the chicken to a cutting board and set aside.

4. Skim any fat from the surface of the cooking liquid. Bring to a boil, uncovered, over high heat. Season the soup with additional salt and pepper. Stir in the noodles and parsley. Reduce the heat to medium and cook, uncovered, until the noodles are tender, about 9 minutes.

5. Cut the chicken into bite-sized pieces. Return to the soup and heat through. Serve hot.

Chicken Rice Soup: Substitute ½ cup long-grain rice for the noodles. Simmer until tender, about 15 minutes.

Straciatella: This makes delicately delicious strands of cheese and egg in the soup. Delete the noodles. In a small bowl, mix 2 large eggs, 2 tablespoons freshly grated Parmesan cheese, and the parsley until well combined. Stirring the simmering soup constantly, drizzle the egg mixture into the soup. Cook uncovered until the strands are set, about 1 minute.

Makes 8 to 12 servings
8 minutes at high pressure

hearty lentil and pasta soup

Pasta e fagioli, literally "pasta and beans," is a thick, stand-your-spoon-up-in-the-pot dish made all over Italy. Arlene makes her version with lentils, which give a hearty bean flavor but need no presoaking. When she used to make it the traditional stove-simmered way, it took a couple of hours. Now with the pressure cooker, it takes under 10 minutes. Leftover soup will thicken upon standing; thin with additional stock or water.

2 tablespoons olive oil

4 ounces pancetta or bacon, coarsely chopped

1 large onion, chopped

4 medium celery ribs, cut into ½-inch dice

5 medium carrots, cut into ½-inch dice

3 garlic cloves, chopped

½ teaspoon dried thyme

½ teaspoon dried oregano

1 bay leaf

1 pound dried lentils, rinsed and sorted to remove stones

One 15-ounce can tomatoes in juice, drained and puréed in a blender

5 cups water

2 cups Homemade Beef Stock (page 24) or canned low-sodium broth

1 teaspoon salt, plus more to taste

¼ teaspoon freshly ground black pepper, plus more to taste

8 ounces small pasta for soup, such as ditalini (1½ cups)

Freshly grated Parmesan cheese, for serving

1. In a 5- to 7-quart pressure cooker, heat the oil over medium heat. Add the pancetta or bacon and cook, turning occasionally, until crisp, about 5 minutes. Using a slotted spoon, transfer the meat to paper towels and set aside.

2. Pour out all but 2 tablespoons of the fat in the pot. Add the onion, celery, carrots, and garlic and cook, stirring occasionally, just until the vegetables begin to soften, about 3 minutes. Stir in the thyme, oregano, and bay leaf. Add the lentils and stir well. Stir in the tomatoes, then the water and stock. Season with 1 teaspoon salt and ¼ teaspoon pepper.

3. Lock the lid in place. Bring to high pressure over high heat. Adjust the heat to maintain pressure. Cook for 8 minutes. Remove from the heat and quick-release the pressure. Open the lid, tilting it away from you to block any escaping steam. Check the lentils for doneness; they should be barely tender. If necessary, simmer, uncovered, until tender. Season the lentils with additional salt and pepper. Stir in the pancetta.

4. Meanwhile, in a large pot of lightly salted water over high heat, cook the pasta until barely tender, about 10 minutes. Drain well.

5. To serve, spoon the pasta into bowls and top with the soup. Serve immediately, with the cheese passed on the side.

Makes 8 to 12 servings
8 minutes at high pressure

minestrone

When we make minestrone, we rarely make it the same way twice, instead improvising with the vegetables in season. For example, when fresh cranberry beans are in season in late summer, we substitute 1 cup of fresh beans for the canned ones and cook the fresh beans with the rest of the vegetables in Step 1. (Late summer is also the time to serve the soup at room temperature, just the way they do in Tuscany during hot weather.) In winter, the soup can be turned into Ribollita (recipe follows). If necessary, omit the fresh basil and add ½ teaspoon dried basil to the soup with the other dried herbs. We encourage you to use this recipe as a springboard for your own version.

7 cups Homemade Chicken Stock (page 23),
   canned low-sodium broth, or water
½ large head escarole, well rinsed and coarsely
   chopped (4 cups)
One 28-ounce can tomatoes in juice, drained and
   coarsely chopped
6 ounces green beans, cut into ½-inch lengths
1 medium onion, chopped
2 medium carrots, cut into ½-inch dice
4 garlic cloves
½ teaspoon salt, plus more to taste
⅛ teaspoon dried oregano
⅛ teaspoon dried rosemary
¼ teaspoon freshly ground black pepper, plus
   more to taste
1 medium zucchini, cut into ½-inch dice
½ cup chopped fresh basil
⅓ cup small pasta for soup, such as ditalini
1 cup dried cannellini (white kidney) beans, soaked,
   cooked, and drained, or one 15-ounce can beans,
   drained and rinsed
Freshly grated Parmesan cheese, for serving

1. In a 5- to 7-quart pressure cooker, combine the stock, escarole, tomatoes, green beans, onion, carrots, garlic, ½ teaspoon salt, oregano, rosemary, and ¼ teaspoon pepper. Lock the lid in place. Bring to high pressure over high heat. Adjust the heat to maintain the pressure. Cook for 10 minutes.

2. Remove from the heat and quick-release the pressure. Open the lid, tilting it away from you to block any escaping steam. Add the zucchini, basil, and pasta. Cook over medium heat, uncovered, until the pasta is tender, about 10 minutes. Add the beans and cook for 1 minute to heat through. Season with additional salt and pepper.

3. Serve hot or cooled to room temperature, with the cheese passed on the side.

Ribollita: Ribollita means "reboiled," so its very name explains that this recipes is a great way to use leftover minestrone. The exact proportions depend on the amount of soup and the size of the baking dish. Preheat the oven to 350°F. Pour half of the soup into a deep baking dish. Top with 4 to 6 slices of toasted crusty Italian bread, then a good sprinkling of freshly grated Parmesan cheese. Repeat with the remaining soup, bread, and cheese, drizzling the top with extra-virgin olive oil. Bake until the soup is simmering and the cheese is golden, 30 to 40 minutes. Serve from the dish.

Makes 8 to 12 servings
10 minutes at high pressure

turkey and root vegetable soup

Are you one of those people who loves to make turkey soup from the carcass of the holiday bird? Well, this soup provides those nostalgic flavors without having to roast a whole turkey first. Frugality is another benefit of this soup, as it uses turkey drumsticks, one of the most inexpensive items in the poultry case. If you have chicken stock or broth, use it, but water also makes a good soup.

3 medium turkey drumsticks (2 pounds total)
1 tablespoon vegetable oil
2 medium leeks, white and pale green parts only,
    chopped, well rinsed, and drained (1 cup)
1 large carrot, cut into ½-inch rounds
1 large parsnip, cut into ½-inch rounds
5 cups Homemade Chicken Stock (page 23),
    canned low-sodium broth, or water
½ teaspoon dried thyme
¼ teaspoon dried rosemary
1 bay leaf
½ teaspoon salt, plus more to taste
¼ teaspoon freshly ground black pepper,
    plus more to taste
2 tablespoons chopped fresh parsley

1. Using a sharp knife, pull the skin from each drumstick, cutting it off at the drumstick knob. Don't bother to remove the skin remaining around the knob.

2. In a 5- to 7-quart pressure cooker, heat the oil over medium heat. In batches, if necessary, add the drumsticks and cook, turning occasionally, until lightly browned, about 5 minutes. Transfer the drumsticks to a plate and set aside.

3. Add the leeks, carrot, and parsnip to the pot and cook, stirring occasionally, until they begin to soften, about 2 minutes. Return the drumsticks to the pot and add the stock, thyme, rosemary, bay leaf, ½ teaspoon salt, and ¼ teaspoon pepper.

4. Lock the lid in place. Bring to high pressure over high heat. Adjust the heat to maintain the pressure. Cook for 30 minutes. Remove the pot from the heat and quick-release the pressure. Open the lid, tilting it away from you to block any escaping steam.

5. Transfer the drumsticks to a cutting board and let cool until easy to handle. Remove the meat from the drumsticks, taking care to discard the long, thin sinews. Coarsely chop the meat into bite-sized pieces and discard the bones and sinews.

6. Skim off any fat on the surface of the soup. Stir in the chopped turkey and parsley. Cook, uncovered, over medium heat, until piping hot, about 3 minutes. Season with additional salt and pepper. Serve hot.

Turkey and Rice Soup: Stir ⅓ cup long-grain rice into the soup with the turkey and parsley. Simmer over medium heat until the rice is tender, about 15 minutes.

Makes 8 to 10 servings
30 minutes at high pressure

provençal onion soup

Rick learned to make this intriguingly seasoned soup at an early-career restaurant job during his college days, and he's been making it ever since. It's a bit different from the one served in Parisian bistros, with tomatoes and a hint of ground cloves flavoring the soup and a bread-and-cheese topping that is applied at the table and not broiled. The pressure cooker doesn't cut down on the time needed to cook the onions until golden and tender, but once that's out of the way, the soup will be finished in less than 10 minutes.

3 tablespoons unsalted butter

2 tablespoons olive oil

4 medium onions, thinly sliced into half-moons (6 cups)

1 garlic clove, finely chopped

¼ teaspoon dried thyme

¼ teaspoon ground cloves

1 bay leaf

½ cup dry white wine

6 cups Homemade Beef Stock (page 24) or canned low-sodium beef broth

One 28-ounce can tomatoes in juice, drained and chopped

½ teaspoon salt, plus more to taste

¼ teaspoon freshly ground black pepper, plus more to taste

Sliced, toasted French bread, for serving

Shredded Gruyère or Swiss cheese, for serving

1. In a 5- to 7-quart pressure cooker, heat the butter and oil over medium-high heat. Add the onions and cook, uncovered, stirring occasionally, until very tender and golden, about 15 minutes. Stir in the garlic, thyme, cloves, and bay leaf and cook for 1 minute.

2. Add the wine and bring to a boil. Stir in the stock, tomatoes, ½ teaspoon salt, and ¼ teaspoon pepper. Lock the lid in place. Bring to high pressure over high heat. Adjust the heat to maintain the pressure. Cook for 6 minutes. Remove from the heat and quick-release the pressure. Open the lid, tilting it away from you to block any escaping steam.

3. Remove the bay leaf. Season the soup with additional salt and pepper. Serve the soup hot, with the bread and cheese on the side, so each person can top the soup with bread and cheese as they wish.

Makes 8 to 10 servings
6 minutes at high pressure

green pea soup with ham

Split pea soup is one of the biggest stumbling blocks for the pressure cooker, because the dried peas create a starchy foam that clogs up the cooker's valves. Arlene takes the attitude that with this deliciously easy pea soup made with frozen peas, who needs to fuss with temperamental split peas? There are lots of variations—we are especially fond of the Curried and Herb versions, which can be served chilled for a light meal on a warm summer's day. One tip: Slice the vegetables quite thin (about 1/8 inch thick or less) so they become tender in 3 minutes of pressure cooking. If they aren't tender, pressure cook again for 1 minute.

1 tablespoon vegetable oil
1/2 cup chopped smoked or boiled ham (see Note)
1 small onion, thinly sliced
1 small carrot, thinly sliced
1 small celery rib with leaves, thinly sliced
1 medium Idaho potato, peeled and very thinly sliced
One 10-ounce package frozen peas (no need to defrost)
2 cups Homemade Chicken Stock (page 23) or canned low-sodium broth
1/2 teaspoon salt, plus more to taste
1/8 teaspoon freshly ground black pepper, plus more to taste
1/4 cup heavy cream

1. In a 5- to 7-quart pressure cooker, heat the oil over medium-high heat. Add the ham and cook until browned, about 5 minutes. Remove the ham with a slotted spoon, leaving any oil in the pot, and set the ham aside.

2. Add the onion, carrot, celery, and potato to the pot. Cook until the vegetables soften, about 2 minutes. Add the frozen peas, stock, 1/2 teaspoon salt, and 1/8 teaspoon pepper. Bring to a boil over high heat. Lock the lid in place. Bring to high pressure over high heat. Adjust the heat to maintain pressure.

3. Cook for 3 minutes. Remove from the heat and quick-release the pressure. Open the lid, tilting it away from you to block any escaping steam. Using a hand-blender, blender, or food processor, purée the soup. Stir in the cream and reserved ham and heat through. Season with additional salt and pepper. Serve hot.

Note: For more ham flavor, make a ham hock stock. Place 1 smoked ham hock, 1 small onion, 1 small carrot (both halved, not chopped), and a pinch of thyme in a pressure cooker. Add 3 cups warm water. Lock the lid in place. Bring to high pressure over high heat. Adjust the heat to maintain pressure. Cook for 20 minutes. Remove the lid. Strain the stock. Remove and discard the skin and bones, and finely chop the ham meat. Substitute the ham stock and its meat for the chicken stock and smoked or boiled ham. You will not have to brown the hock meat in oil, as it will be more flavorful than delicatessen ham.

Curried Green Pea Soup: Delete the ham. In Step 2, after the vegetables are softened, add 1 1/4 teaspoons curry powder and stir until it releases its aroma, about 30 seconds. Serve warm or chilled.

Green Pea Soup with Fresh Herbs: Delete the ham. Stir 1 tablespoon finely chopped fresh mint, dill, or tarragon into the soup. If desired, top each serving with a drizzle of additional heavy cream and a pinch of chopped fresh herbs. Serve warm or chilled.

──────────

Makes 4 to 6 servings
3 minutes at high pressure

zucchini and mushroom soup

This light but creamy soup with the herbaceous flavor of fresh dill will become a secret weapon in your artillery of quick-and-easy recipes. A food processor makes fast work of shredding the zucchini and chopping the mushrooms. With those chores out of the way, the pressure cooker will make the soup in minutes, one that is sophisticated enough for company yet homey enough for a satisfying weekend lunch.

2 tablespoons unsalted butter
1 large onion, chopped
12 ounces white mushrooms, chopped
2 garlic cloves, minced
6 small (1½ pounds) zucchini, trimmed and shredded
1 tablespoon sweet Hungarian paprika
4½ cups Homemade Chicken Stock (page 23) or canned low-sodium chicken broth
½ teaspoon salt, plus more to taste
¼ teaspoon freshly ground black pepper, plus more to taste
¼ cup all-purpose flour
1½ tablespoons chopped fresh dill
Sour cream, for serving

1. In a 5- to 7-quart pressure cooker, melt the butter over medium heat. Add the onion and cook until softened, about 2 minutes. Add the mushrooms and garlic and cook until the mushrooms begin to soften, about 2 minutes. Stir in the zucchini and paprika. Add 4 cups of the stock, and ½ teaspoon salt and ¼ teaspoon pepper.

2. Lock the lid in place. Bring to high pressure over high heat. Adjust the heat to maintain the pressure. Cook for 8 minutes. Remove from the heat and quick-release the pressure. Open the lid, tilting it away from you to block any escaping steam.

3. Place the uncovered pressure cooker over medium-low heat and bring the soup to a simmer. In a medium bowl, whisk the remaining ½ cup stock and the flour until smooth. Whisk into the soup. Simmer until the soup is thickened and no trace of raw flour flavor remains, about 5 minutes. Stir in the dill, and season with additional salt and pepper.

4. Serve hot, topping each serving with a dollop of sour cream.

Zucchini and Wild Mushroom Soup: Dried mushrooms cook quickly in a pressure cooker without soaking. Rinse ½ cup (½ ounce) dried porcini mushrooms under cold running water to remove any grit. Add the rinsed mushrooms to the soup with the fresh mushrooms.

Makes 8 to 12 servings
8 minutes at high pressure

meat main courses

Few foods are as satisfying and comforting as a meat stew. But the busier we get, the less time we have to cook those delicious stews, ragouts, pot roasts, and chilis. Other casualties of the "cook it quick" craze are tough meats that need long simmering to become tender and succulent. How can we turn our backs on such favorites as lamb and veal shanks, corned beef, beef brisket, and veal breast?

Thanks to the pressure cooker, you'll never have to scurry to find the time to cook these mouthwatering dishes again. The steam and pressure combine to tenderize tough meats in a fraction of their traditional cooking times. With a little attention to detail (and a good kitchen timer), even tender chops and roasts can be prepared in the pressure cooker.

tips for meats

> In general, tough cuts of meat (beef chuck, bottom round, brisket, shanks, and short ribs; lamb shanks and shoulder; veal breast, shoulder, and osso bucco; pork ribs and shoulder) work best in the pressure cooker. Leaner, more tender cuts, such as pork loin and pork and lamb chops, can be prepared in the pressure cooker if cooked at reduced times to avoid overcooking and drying out.

> Avoid generic meats labeled "stewing meat," because you never know what cut of meat you're getting. Even if you buy a specific cut of cubed meat, such as chuck, most butchers tend to cube them too small. Buy the specific roast and cut it into pieces about 1½-inch square. Smaller cubes can easily overcook and get mushy and stringy.

> When browning batches of cubed meat for a stew in the cooker, save time by browning some of the cubes in a separate skillet. If desired, pour 1 cup of the cooking liquid (broth, wine, or water) into the skillet and scrape up any browned bits with a wooden spoon; use this liquid as part of the required amount in the recipe.

> When seasoning meats with salt and pepper, combine the two seasonings in a small bowl; this mixture seasons the meat much more evenly than using each condiment separately.

> When tying large cuts of meat, leave two 12-inch lengths of string hanging from both ends. Use the strings to lift and turn the meat—you won't need a meat fork, which pierces the meat and releases juices.

> Most of our recipes are cooked in a liquid. The fat from the meat is transferred to the liquid and should be removed. Let the cooking liquid stand off the heat for a few minutes to allow the fat to rise to the top, and use a large spoon to skim it off.

> Some of the meat recipes use relatively small amounts of liquid. If necessary, increase the liquid to meet your cooker's minimum liquid requirement. Before making a gravy, pour off some of the cooking liquid. Gradually add the thickening ingredient to get the desired thickness.

➤ Pressure cooking adds steam to the food, which can dilute the flavor of the cooking liquid. This is easily remedied by boiling the skimmed cooking liquid for a few minutes to concentrate the flavors.

➤ If the recipe calls for wine, use a good, drinkable brand—never use "cooking wine," which is made from inferior wine and heavily salted. To disperse any alcohol flavors that could intensify in the cooker, add the wine to the pot right after cooking the seasoning vegetables, and allow it to come to a boil before adding the other ingredients.

➤ When thickening a sauce with dissolved cornstarch or *beurre manie* (a flour-and-butter paste), remember that the liquid must come to a boil in order to activate the thickening. Cornstarch-thickened sauces will thicken almost immediately, if added to simmering liquid. Simmer sauces thickened with *beurre manie* for about 5 minutes to remove any raw flour taste. If a sauce seems too thick, thin with broth or water. If it is too thin, add more dissolved cornstarch (even if it was originally thickened with *beurre manie*).

➤ Let roasts stand for at least 10 minutes before slicing. This allows the juices to settle and makes for easier slicing.

➤ In meat-and-bean dishes, such as chili, cook the beans separately and add them to the meat just before serving. It is difficult to guess the cooking time of dried beans, and you can easily overcook the meat while trying to get the beans tender.

rolled butterflied leg of lamb

When company is coming and you're short on time, make this extraordinary stuffed leg of lamb. Time it carefully to ensure medium-rare meat.

One 3-pound boneless leg of lamb, rolled and tied
¼ teaspoon salt, plus more to taste
¼ teaspoon freshly ground black pepper, plus more to taste
2 tablespoons drained and chopped sun-dried tomatoes in oil
2 tablespoons chopped fresh parsley
1 teaspoon chopped fresh rosemary or ½ teaspoon dried rosemary
1 garlic clove, finely chopped
1 tablespoon olive oil
¾ cup hearty red wine, such as Zinfandel
¾ cup Homemade Beef Stock (page 24) or canned low-sodium broth
2 tablespoons water
1½ tablespoons cornstarch
1 tablespoon Dijon mustard (optional)

1. Untie the roast and open it up on the work surface. Using a sharp knife, cut one or two flaps of the meat almost parallel to the work surface. Open up the flaps like a book.

2. In a small bowl, mix ¼ teaspoon salt and ¼ teaspoon pepper. Season the meat with half of the mixture. Sprinkle with the sun-dried tomatoes, parsley, rosemary, and garlic. Roll up the lamb. Using kitchen twine, tie crosswise at 2-inch intervals, then lengthwise. Season the outside of the meat with the remaining salt-and-pepper mixture.

3. In a 5- to 7-quart pressure cooker, heat the oil over medium-high heat. Add the lamb and cook, turning occasionally, until lightly browned, about 4 minutes. Transfer the lamb to a plate and set aside.

4. Add the wine and bring to a boil, stirring up the browned bits on the bottom of the pot with a wooden spoon. Stir in the broth. Return the lamb to the cooker.

5. Lock the lid in place. Bring to high pressure over high heat. Adjust the heat to maintain the pressure. Cook for 20 minutes. Remove from the heat and quick-release the pressure. Open the lid, tilting it away from you to block any escaping steam. Insert a meat thermometer in the center of the lamb. It should read 115° to 120°F. The internal temperature of the lamb will rise 5° to 10°F while standing. Transfer the lamb to a carving board and let stand for 10 minutes. Let the cooking liquid stand for 5 minutes.

6. Skim off any fat from the surface of the cooking liquid. Return the pot to medium heat and bring to a simmer. Place the water in a small bowl, sprinkle with the cornstarch, and stir to dissolve. Stir into the simmering broth and cook until thickened. Remove from the heat and whisk in the mustard. Season with additional salt and pepper.

7. Remove the strings, carve the lamb, and serve with the sauce on the side.

Makes 6 to 8 servings
20 minutes at high pressure

lamb and white bean ragout

Lamb shoulder is a versatile cut of meat and makes a tasty, hearty stew. You may have to order it ahead from your butcher—most shoulder is automatically cut into chops. If you wish, substitute 3½ pounds of bone-in lamb neck for the shoulder, increasing the cooking time to 15 minutes. (You will have to deal with the bones while eating, but they add a lot of flavor to the stew.) If you have Demi-Glace Rapide (page 27), stir one cube into the finished sauce.

2 tablespoons olive oil
2½ pounds boneless lamb shoulder, trimmed of
    excess fat, cut into 1½-inch pieces
½ teaspoon salt, plus more to taste
¼ teaspoon freshly ground black pepper, plus more
    to taste
1 large onion, chopped
3 medium carrots, cut into 1-inch lengths
2 garlic cloves, minced
1 cup dry white wine
One 14½-ounce can tomatoes in juice, drained
    and chopped
¼ teaspoon dried rosemary
¼ teaspoon dried thyme
Pinch of ground cinnamon
Pinch of ground cloves
1 bay leaf
2 tablespoons cold water
1 tablespoon cornstarch
1½ cups dried cannellini (white kidney) beans,
    soaked, cooked, and drained, (page 92), or two
    15-ounce cans cannellini beans, drained and rinsed
4 ounces feta cheese, crumbled
Chopped fresh parsley or rosemary, for garnish

1. In a 5- to 7-quart pressure cooker, heat 1 tablespoon oil over medium-high heat. In batches, add the lamb and cook, turning occasionally, until lightly browned, about 4 minutes. Transfer to a plate, season with ½ teaspoon salt and ¼ teaspoon pepper, and set aside.

2. Add the remaining 1 tablespoon oil to the pot and return to medium heat. Add the onion, carrots, and garlic. Cook, stirring often, until the vegetables begin to soften, about 2 minutes. Add the wine, and stir to scrape up the browned bits on the bottom of the pot with a wooden spoon. Add the tomatoes, rosemary, thyme, cinnamon, cloves, and bay leaf. Return the lamb and any juices on the plate to the pot.

3. Lock the lid in place. Bring to high pressure over high heat. Adjust the heat to maintain the pressure. Cook for 20 minutes. Remove from the heat and quick-release the pressure. Open the lid, tilting it away from you to block any escaping steam.

4. Let stand for 5 minutes. Skim off any fat that rises to the surface. Return the pot to medium heat and bring to a simmer. Place the water in a small bowl, sprinkle with the cornstarch, and stir to dissolve. Stir into the simmering broth and cook until thickened. Stir in the white beans and cook until heated through, about 2 minutes. Season with additional salt and pepper.

5. Transfer to a deep serving bowl. Sprinkle with the feta and parsley or rosemary, and serve immediately.

Makes 4 to 6 servings
20 minutes at high pressure

MEAT MAIN COURSES

46

lamb shanks with garlic sauce

Many chefs have recently put humble lamb shanks at center stage on their restaurant menus. Let them braise it for hours—with a pressure cooker, the home cook can prepare shanks in under an hour. This garlic sauce is a great way to accent the delectable meat.

½ teaspoon salt
¼ teaspoon dried rosemary
¼ teaspoon dried thyme
¼ teaspoon freshly ground black pepper
Four 1¼-pound lamb shanks
2 tablespoons extra-virgin olive oil
8 garlic cloves, crushed under a chef's knife
 and peeled
1 cup dry white wine
½ cup Homemade Beef Stock (page 24) or
 canned low-sodium broth

1. In a small bowl, rub the salt, rosemary, thyme, and pepper between your fingertips to crush the herbs (or use a mortar and pestle). Sprinkle all over the shanks.

2. In a 5- to 7-quart pressure cooker, heat 1 tablespoon of the oil over medium-high heat. In batches, add the shanks and cook, turning occasionally, until lightly browned, about 3 minutes. Transfer the shanks to a plate and set aside.

3. Remove the cooker from the heat to cool slightly. Return to medium heat. Add the remaining 1 tablespoon oil and the garlic. Stir until the garlic is barely beginning to color, about 1 minute. Immediately add the wine. Bring to a boil, scraping up the browned bits on the bottom of the cooker with a wooden spoon. Add the stock. Return the shanks to the cooker.

4. Lock the lid in place. Bring to high pressure over high heat. Adjust the heat to maintain the pressure. Cook for 20 minutes. Remove from the heat and quick-release the pressure. Open the lid, tilting it away from you to block any escaping steam. Switch the positions of the shanks from top to bottom. Cover again, bring to high pressure, and cook for an additional 20 minutes. Transfer the shanks to a serving platter and cover with aluminum foil to keep warm.

5. Let the cooking liquid stand for about 5 minutes. Skim off any fat from the surface. Uncovered, bring to a boil over high heat. Cook, uncovered, until the liquid is evaporated by about half, about 5 minutes, whisking occasionally to help dissolve the garlic. Pour the sauce over the shanks and serve immediately.

Makes 4 servings
Two 20-minute periods at high pressure

loin lamb chops dijonnaise

MEAT MAIN COURSES

This is the recipe of Arlene's that made Rick a pressure-cooker convert. The trick is to use thick-cut lamb chops—regular, thin-cut chops will overcook. You'll have to ask your butcher to cut them specially for you—some butchers may balk at the thickness, but instruct them to do as you ask. The timing depends on the doneness of the meat. We find that 3 minutes of pressure cooking yields a perfect, medium-rare chop. One chop will be enough for delicate appetites, but you can stack up to six chops in the cooker, if you wish, as long as you don't go higher than two-thirds of the height of the pot.

Four 8-ounce loin lamb chops, cut 2 inches
thick
1 tablespoon olive oil
2 garlic cloves, crushed and peeled
2 quarter-sized pieces fresh ginger, unpeeled
4 sprigs fresh rosemary or 1 teaspoon dried
rosemary
1/8 teaspoon salt, plus more to taste
1/8 teaspoon freshly ground black pepper, plus
more to taste
1/4 cup hearty red wine, such as Zinfandel
2 tablespoons Homemade Beef Stock (page
24), canned low-sodium broth, or water
(see Note)
1 tablespoon Dijon mustard
1/2 teaspoon Japanese soy sauce

1. Trim and discard the fat from the perimeter of each chop. In a 5- to 7-quart pressure cooker, heat the oil over medium-high heat until very hot but not smoking. Add the chops and brown the underside, about 2 minutes. Turn the chops, add the garlic and ginger to the pot, and brown the other side. Transfer the chops to a plate. Place a rosemary sprig on each chop or sprinkle each with 1/4 teaspoon of the dried rosemary. Season with 1/8 teaspoon salt and 1/8 teaspoon pepper.

2. Working quickly, add the red wine to the pot, then place the rack in the pot. Place the chops on the rack. Lock the lid in place. Bring to high pressure over high heat. (If the cooker doesn't come up to pressure, add 1/4 cup water.) Cook for 3 minutes. Remove from the heat and quick-release the pressure. Open the lid, tilting it away from you to block any escaping steam. Using kitchen tongs, transfer the chops to a serving platter.

3. Discard the ginger, but keep the garlic in the pot. Add the stock, mustard, and soy sauce. Bring to a boil over high heat, crushing the garlic into the sauce. Cook just until thickened, about 30 seconds (or slightly longer if you added water to the cooker). Season with additional salt and pepper. Pour the sauce over the chops. Serve immediately.

Note: If desired, substitute 2 tablespoons Demi-Glace Rapide (page 27) or store-bought veal demi-glace for the beef stock. It gives the sauce an incredible finesse.

Makes 2 to 4 servings
3 minutes at high pressure

boeuf bourguignonne

This rich beef ragout is a perfect example of the best of pressure cooking. It has all the flavor of a long-simmered version, but is made in much less time. Serve with noodles or garlic-flavored mashed potatoes.

1 tablespoon olive oil
3 bacon strips, coarsely chopped
3 pounds beef bottom round, cut into 1½-inch pieces
½ teaspoon salt, plus more to taste
¼ teaspoon freshly ground black pepper, plus more to taste
10 ounces fresh white mushrooms, each cut lengthwise into quarters
4 medium carrots, cut into 1-inch lengths
½ cup chopped shallots
2 garlic cloves
1 cup hearty red wine, such as Zinfandel
2 cups Homemade Beef Stock (page 24), or canned low-sodium broth
1 tablespoon tomato paste
4 tablespoons (½ stick) unsalted butter, at room temperature
¼ cup all-purpose flour

1. In a 5- to 7-quart pressure cooker, heat the oil over medium heat. Add the bacon and cook, stirring occasionally, until the bacon is crisp and browned, about 5 minutes. Transfer the bacon to paper towels to drain. Pour the bacon fat into a small bowl. Return 1 tablespoon of the fat to the cooker, reserving the remaining fat.

2. Heat the fat over medium-high heat. In batches, adding more fat as needed, add the beef and cook, turning occasionally, until browned, about 4 minutes. Transfer the beef to a plate. Season the beef with ½ teaspoon salt and ¼ teaspoon pepper and set aside.

3. Pour 1 tablespoon of the reserved fat (or additional oil, if the fat has been depleted) into the cooker. Reduce the heat to medium. Add the mushrooms, carrots, shallots, and garlic. Cook, stirring occasionally, until the mushrooms soften, about 5 minutes. Add the wine. Bring to a boil, scraping up any browned bits on the bottom of the pan with a wooden spoon. Stir in the broth and tomato paste. Return the beef and any juices on the plate to the cooker.

4. Lock the lid in place. Bring to high pressure over high heat. Adjust the heat to maintain the pressure. Cook for 20 minutes. Remove from the heat and quick-release the pressure. Open the lid, tilting it away from you to block any escaping steam. Stir in the reserved bacon. Using a large skimmer or slotted spoon, transfer the meat and vegetables to a deep serving bowl. Cover with aluminum foil to keep warm. Let the liquid stand for 5 minutes.

5. Skim any fat from the surface of the cooking liquid. Bring to a boil, uncovered, over medium-high heat. In a medium bowl, using a rubber spatula, work the butter and flour together until smooth. Gradually whisk about 1 cup of the cooking liquid into the flour mixture to make a thin paste. Briskly whisk the paste into the boiling liquid. Cook, stirring occasionally, until the sauce is thickened and no trace of raw flour taste remains, about 5 minutes. Season with additional salt and pepper. Pour the sauce over the meat and vegetables, stir gently, and serve.

Makes 6 to 8 servings
20 minutes at high pressure

abilene **beef** and **bean chili**

There is a chili recipe for every cook in Texas. Some folks top their chili with shredded cheese, onions, and sour cream, but others think that kind of behavior should be reserved for an ice cream sundae, and want their chili naked. Beans are even more controversial: Some like them, yet some wouldn't be caught dead with legumes in their pot. One thing for sure: Most agree that tomatoes don't belong anywhere near the chili.

Base your decisions on your mood and what's in the cupboard. Cooking the beans with the meat often ends up with one of the two being under- or over-cooked. To play it safe, cook them separately, and stir them together at the end.

2 tablespoons olive oil, plus more as needed
2 pounds beef bottom round, cut into 1½-inch
   pieces
1 large onion, chopped
1 medium red bell pepper, seeded and chopped
1 jalapeño chile, seeded and finely chopped
3 garlic cloves, finely chopped
2 tablespoons chili powder
½ teaspoon salt, plus more to taste
2 cups Homemade Beef Stock (page 24) or
   canned low-sodium broth
¼ cup yellow cornmeal
1½ cups (12 ounces) dried pinto beans, soaked,
   drained, and cooked (see page 92), or two
   15-ounce cans pinto beans, rinsed and drained

1. In a 5- to 7-quart pressure cooker, heat 1 tablespoon of the oil over medium-high heat. In batches, add the beef and cook, adding more oil as needed, turning occasionally, until browned, about 4 minutes. Transfer to a plate and set aside.

2. Pour out any fat in the cooker. Add the remaining 1 tablespoon oil and heat. Add the onion, red pepper, jalapeño, and garlic. Cook, stirring often, until the vegetables begin to soften, about 2 minutes. Add the reserved beef and any juices from the plate, and sprinkle with the chili powder and salt. Mix well. Stir in the stock, scraping up any browned bits on the bottom of the cooker.

3. Lock the lid in place. Bring to high pressure over high heat. Adjust the temperature to maintain the heat. Cook for 20 minutes. Remove from the heat and quick-release the pressure. Open the lid, tilting it away from you to block any escaping steam. Let the chili stand for 5 minutes.

4. Skim any fat from the surface of the chili. In a small bowl, whisk about 1 cup of the cooking liquid into the cornmeal to make a paste. Stir the cornmeal mixture into the chili, and add the beans. Cook, stirring often, until the juices are thickened, 3 to 5 minutes, taking care that the chili doesn't stick and scorch on the bottom of the cooker. Season with additional salt to taste. Serve immediately.

▬▬▬▬▬▬

Makes 8 servings
20 minutes at high pressure

old-fashioned **beef** stew with carrots and potatoes

While all cooks have their own way to make beef stew, this one has the makings of an American classic. It is simply flavored with thyme and bay leaf, chunky with beef, carrots, and potatoes (substitute parsnips or turnips, if you like, or add other vegetables), and served with a rich brown sauce.

2 tablespoons vegetable oil, plus more as needed
2½ pounds beef chuck roast, cut into 1½-inch pieces
½ teaspoon salt, plus more to taste
¼ teaspoon freshly ground black pepper, plus more to taste
1 large onion, chopped
2 garlic cloves, finely chopped
2 cups Homemade Beef Stock (page 24) or canned low-sodium broth
1 tablespoon tomato paste
½ teaspoon dried thyme
1 bay leaf
4 medium carrots, cut into 1-inch lengths
4 medium (1 pound) red-skinned potatoes, scrubbed, cut into 1-inch pieces
3 tablespoons unsalted butter, at room temperature
3 tablespoons all-purpose flour

1. In a 5- to 7-quart pressure cooker, heat 1 tablespoon of the oil over medium-high heat. In batches, adding more oil as needed, add the beef and cook, turning occasionally, until browned, about 4 minutes. Transfer the beef to a plate. Season the beef with ½ teaspoon salt and ¼ teaspoon pepper and set aside. Pour off the fat in the cooker.

2. Add the remaining 1 tablespoon oil to the cooker and heat over medium heat. Add the onion and garlic. Cook, stirring occasionally, until the onion begins to soften, about 2 minutes. Stir in the stock, tomato paste, thyme, and bay leaf. Return the beef and any juices on the plate to the cooker.

3. Lock the lid in place. Bring to high pressure over high heat. Adjust the heat to maintain the pressure. Cook for 20 minutes. Remove from the heat and quick-release the pressure. Open the lid, tilting it away from you to block any escaping steam. Let the stew stand for 5 minutes.

4. Skim off any fat from the surface of the cooking liquid. Add the carrots and potatoes. Replace the lid and bring the stew back to high pressure over high heat. Cook for 5 minutes. Remove from the heat, quick-release the pressure, and remove the lid. Using a large skimmer or slotted spoon, transfer the meat and vegetables to a deep serving bowl and cover with aluminum foil to keep warm.

5. Bring the cooking liquid, uncovered, back to a boil over medium-high heat. In a medium bowl, using a rubber spatula, work the butter and flour together until smooth. Gradually whisk about 1 cup of the cooking liquid into the flour mixture to make a thin paste. Briskly whisk into the boiling liquid. Cook, stirring occasionally, until the sauce is thickened and no trace of raw flour taste remains, about 5 minutes. Season with additional salt and pepper. Pour the sauce over the meat and vegetables, stir gently, and serve.

Makes 6 servings
20 minutes at high pressure for meat,
then 5 minutes at high pressure for vegetables

MEAT MAIN COURSES

cuban pot roast with capers and olives

Because the strips of vegetables look like tattered fabric, this is often called *ropa vieja,* Spanish for "old clothes." That's an impoverished name for a dish that tastes like a million bucks. Serve spooned over rice that has been cooked with a generous pinch of saffron in the cooking liquid.

1 tablespoon vegetable oil
2 pounds (¾-inch thick) beef chuck steaks, cut into 4 or 6 pieces to fit the cooker
½ teaspoon salt
¼ teaspoon freshly ground black pepper
1 medium onion, cut into ½-inch-thick half-moons
1 medium carrot, cut into ½-inch-thick rounds
1 medium red bell pepper, seeded, cut into ½-inch-thick strips
2 garlic cloves, finely chopped
One 28-ounce can tomatoes in juice, drained and chopped
1 cup Homemade Beef Stock (page 24) or canned low-sodium broth
½ teaspoon dried oregano
Pinch of cinnamon
¼ cup chopped pimiento-stuffed green olives
2 tablespoons bottled capers, rinsed

1. In a 5- to 7-quart pressure cooker, heat the oil over medium heat. In batches, add the beef and cook, turning once, until browned on both sides, about 4 minutes. Transfer to a plate. Season with the salt and pepper and set aside.

2. Add the onion, carrot, red pepper, and garlic to the cooker. Cook, stirring often, until the vegetables begin to soften, about 2 minutes. Add the tomatoes, stock, oregano, and cinnamon, stirring to scrape up any browned bits on the bottom of the cooker. Return the beef and any juices on the plate to the cooker.

3. Lock the lid in place. Bring to high pressure over high heat. Adjust the heat to maintain the pressure. Cook for 20 minutes. Remove from the heat and quick-release the pressure. Open the lid, tilting it away from you to block any escaping steam. Transfer the meat to a serving platter and cover with aluminum foil to keep warm.

4. Let the cooking liquid stand for about 5 minutes. Skim off any fat from the surface of the cooking liquid. Add the olives and capers. Cook, uncovered, over high heat, until the mixture is slightly thickened, 3 to 5 minutes. Pour over the meat and serve immediately.

━━━━━━━━━━

Makes 4 to 6 servings
20 minutes at high pressure

pot roast à la **française**

When you say *pot-au-feu* in France, it means much more than pot roast, or even its literal translation of "pot on the fire." The beef and vegetables are simmered until tender, but they are reserved until the cooking broth is bolstered with pasta and served as a light first course. Admittedly, *pot-au-feu* usually contains more than one cut of beef, along with sausages, chicken, and just about whatever else you can fit into a huge stockpot. In the pressure cooker's case, the limitation of size just means that the dish is more accessible to the American palate. Serve the roast in the French style, with coarse salt, freshly ground black pepper, and Dijon mustard. This is one dish that is much better when prepared with homemade beef broth, as the cooking broth must be delicious.

1 tablespoon vegetable oil
One 3½-pound beef bottom round roast, tied
½ teaspoon salt, plus more to taste
¼ teaspoon freshly ground black pepper, plus more to taste
3 cups Homemade Beef Stock (page 24) or high-quality frozen beef stock (available at some supermarkets, and specialty grocers)
1 pound red-skinned potatoes, cut into 1-inch pieces
2 medium carrots, cut into 1-inch lengths
2 medium parsnips, cut into 1-inch lengths
⅓ cup small pasta, such as ditalini, cooked
2 tablespoons chopped parsley, for garnish
Freshly grated Parmesan cheese, for serving the broth
Coarse salt, freshly ground black pepper, and Dijon mustard, for serving

1. In a 5- to 7-quart pressure cooker, heat the oil over medium-high heat. Season the beef with ½ teaspoon salt and ¼ teaspoon pepper. Place in the pressure cooker and brown on all sides, about 5 minutes. Transfer the beef to a plate. Pour off any fat in the pot. Return the beef to the pot and pour in the stock.

2. Lock the lid in place. Bring to high pressure over high heat. Adjust the heat to maintain the pressure. Cook for 1¼ hours.

3. Meanwhile, preheat the oven to 200°F. Remove the pressure cooker from the heat and quick-release the pressure. Open the lid, tilting it away from you to block any escaping steam. Using a slotted spoon, transfer the beef and a ladleful of the cooking liquid to a deep, heat-proof serving bowl. Cover tightly with aluminum foil and keep warm in the oven.

4. Skim any fat from the surface of the cooking liquid. Add the potatoes, carrots, and parsnips to the pot. Lock the lid in place. Bring to high pressure over high heat. Cook for 5 minutes. Remove from the heat and quick-release the pressure. Using the slotted spoon, transfer the vegetables to the platter with the beef, cover, and return to the oven to keep warm.

5. Stir the cooked pasta and parsley into the broth. Season with additional salt and pepper. Serve hot in soup bowls, passing the Parmesan on the side.

6. To serve the meat and vegetables, transfer the roast to a carving board. Remove the strings and carve the meat. Return to the bowl and serve immediately, with the salt, pepper, and mustard.

Makes 6 to 8 servings
1¼ hours at high pressure for the meat,
then 5 minutes at high pressure for the vegetables

yankee pot roast

A basic pot roast recipe with clear-eyed, Yankee simplicity that can be embellished with vegetables or herbs, if you wish. Serve it with mashed potatoes.

1 tablespoon vegetable oil
One 3-pound rump roast, trimmed, but leaving the fat "cap" intact
½ teaspoon salt, plus more to taste
¼ teaspoon freshly ground black pepper, plus more to taste
1 medium onion, sliced into ¼-inch-thick half-moons
2 bay leaves
2 cups Homemade Beef Stock (page 24), canned low-sodium broth, or water
2 tablespoons unsalted butter, at room temperature
2 tablespoons all-purpose flour

1. In a 5- to 7-quart pressure cooker, heat the oil over medium-high heat. Season the roast with ½ teaspoon salt and ¼ teaspoon pepper. Add the roast to the pressure cooker, fat side down. Cook, turning occasionally, until browned on all sides, about 6 minutes. Transfer the roast to a plate. Pour off all but 1 tablespoon of the fat from the pot. Add the onion and cook until softened, about 3 minutes. Add the bay leaves.

2. Pour in the stock, scraping up any browned bits on the bottom of the pot with a wooden spoon. Return the roast to the pot. Lock the lid in place. Bring to high pressure over high heat. Adjust the heat to maintain the pressure. Cook for 1 hour.

Remove from the heat and quick-release the steam. Open the lid, tilting it away from you to block any escaping steam. Transfer the roast to a serving platter and cover loosely with foil to keep warm.

3. Remove the bay leaves from the cooking liquid and let the liquid stand for 5 minutes. Skim the fat from the top of the cooking liquid. In a small bowl, using a rubber spatula, work the butter and flour together until smooth. Whisk 1 cup of the cooking liquid into the butter/flour mixture to make a thin paste. Return the uncovered pot to the stove and bring the skimmed cooking liquid to a boil over medium heat. Whisk in the paste and cook until the liquid reduces slightly and thickens into a light-bodied gravy, about 6 minutes. Season with additional salt and pepper.

4. Slice the roast. Pour about half of the gravy over the meat. Pour the remaining sauce in a sauceboat and pass with the meat.

Makes 6 servings
1 hour at high pressure

italian pot roast

The Italians' special way with pot roast (called *stracotto*) is typical of their way of cooking—using just a few ingredients, simply prepared, but bursting with flavor. This makes plenty of sauce for spooning over pasta or rice. In fact, you could serve it the way they do in Italy, tossing most of the sauce with a pound of pasta for the first course, then offering sliced meat as a main course with the remaining sauce.

2 tablespoons olive oil
One 3¼-pound boneless rump or bottom round roast
½ teaspoon salt
¼ teaspoon freshly ground black pepper
1 large onion, chopped
2 medium carrots, chopped
2 medium celery ribs, chopped
2 garlic cloves, finely chopped
½ cup dry red wine
One 28-ounce can tomatoes in juice, drained, juices reserved, and chopped

1. In a 5- to 7-quart pressure cooker, heat 1 tablespoon of the oil over medium-high heat. Add the roast and cook, turning occasionally, until lightly browned on all sides, about 4 minutes. Transfer to a plate and season with the salt and pepper.

2. Pour off the fat in the pressure cooker. Add the remaining 1 tablespoon oil and heat over medium heat. Add the onion, carrots, celery, and garlic. Cook, stirring occasionally, until the vegetables begin to soften, about 2 minutes. Add the wine and bring to a boil, scraping up the browned bits on the bottom of the pan with a wooden spoon. Add the chopped tomatoes and their juices.

3. Return the meat and any juices on the plate to the cooker. Lock the lid in place. Bring to high pressure over high heat. Adjust the heat to maintain the pressure. Cook for 1¼ hours. Remove from the heat and quick-release the pressure. Open the lid, tilting it away from you to block any escaping steam. Transfer the roast to a serving platter and let stand for 10 minutes.

4. Skim any fat from the surface of the sauce. Slice the meat and serve with the sauce.

Makes 4 to 6 servings
1¼ hours at high pressure

corned beef boiled dinner

If there's one day of the year when corned beef and cabbage makes an appearance, it is, of course, St. Patrick's Day. But, if the holiday falls on a weekday, most cooks are hard-pressed to cook the traditional meal—it just takes too long! With a pressure cooker, the cooking time is more than cut in half. This is not your typical ho-hum boiled dinner; beer and spices give the cooking liquid a delicious depth of flavor. Serve with mustard and prepared horseradish sauce.

One 3-pound corned beef brisket with pickling spice packet (see Note)
2 cups water
One 12-ounce bottle of lager beer
2 medium onions, peeled and cut in half lengthwise
2 garlic cloves, peeled and crushed
4 medium (1 pound) red-skinned potatoes, scrubbed but unpeeled, cut into 1-inch pieces
4 medium carrots, cut into 1-inch lengths
1 small (2 pounds) head green cabbage, cut into 6 wedges

1. Rinse the corned beef, but do not trim the fat. Tie the spices in a double thickness of cheesecloth.

2. Place the rack in a 5- to 7-quart pressure cooker. Add the water, beer, onions, garlic, and spice sachet. Place the corned beef in the pot (don't worry if it touches the sides—it will shrink during cooking).

3. Lock the lid in place. Bring to high pressure over high heat. Adjust the heat to maintain the pressure. Cook for 1 hour, 10 minutes. Let the steam release naturally (about 15 minutes). Open the lid, tilting it away from you to block any escaping steam.

4. Transfer the meat to a serving platter. Using a slotted spoon, transfer the onions to a large serving bowl. Cover both with aluminum foil to keep warm.

5. Place the potatoes and carrots in the cooking liquid in the pot. (The nitrates in the corned beef will probably have turned the liquid red, but don't be concerned.) Place the cabbage on top, trying to submerge it in the broth as much as possible. Lock the lid in place. Bring to high pressure over high heat. Adjust the heat to maintain the pressure. Cook for 6 minutes. Using a mesh skimmer or slotted spoon, transfer the vegetables to the serving bowl.

6. Slice the corned beef across the grain. Serve, with the vegetables passed on the side.

Note: Most corned beef comes packaged with a separate packet of pickling spices. If yours doesn't, substitute ½ teaspoon yellow mustard seeds, ½ teaspoon whole black peppercorns, 6 whole allspice berries, 6 whole cloves, and 1 crumbled bay leaf. If your corned beef is coated with spices, rinse them off under cold running water, as the free-floating spices could clog the vent.

Makes 4 to 6 servings
1 hour, 10 minutes at high pressure for the beef, then 6 minutes at high pressure for the vegetables

deviled short ribs

S hort ribs are surely one of the most succulent ways to enjoy beef. Our recipe renders out their fat, leaving it behind in the cooking liquid. (You won't use the liquid in this dish, but it should be reserved and used as beef broth at another meal.) The ribs are spread with spicy mustard, coated with crumbs, and baked quickly to give them a crunchy crust. Hold out on making this dish until you find meaty short ribs—some butchers put out ribs that Fido might like, but don't have enough meat on them for hungry humans.

2 tablespoons olive oil
4 pounds meaty beef short ribs
¼ teaspoon salt
1 medium onion, chopped
1 medium carrot, chopped
3 garlic cloves, crushed under a knife and peeled
2 cups water
¼ teaspoon dried thyme
¼ teaspoon whole black peppercorns
1 bay leaf

Nonstick cooking oil spray

DEVILED CRUST
6 tablespoons Dijon mustard
1 garlic clove, crushed through a press
⅛ teaspoon ground hot red pepper flakes
2 cups fresh Italian or French bread crumbs
   (make in a blender or food processor)
2 tablespoons olive oil

1. In a 5- to 7-quart pressure cooker, heat 1 tablespoon of the oil over medium-high heat. In batches, add the short ribs and cook, turning occasionally, until lightly browned, about 3 minutes. Transfer the ribs to a plate, season with the salt, and set aside.

2. Pour off any fat in the cooker. Return the cooker to medium heat. Add the remaining 1 tablespoon oil. Add the onion, carrot, and garlic. Cook, stirring often, until the vegetables begin to soften, about 2 minutes. Add the water, scraping up the browned bits on the bottom of the cooker with a wooden spoon. Add the thyme, peppercorns, and bay leaf. Return the ribs to the cooker.

3. Lock the lid in place. Bring to high pressure over high heat. Adjust the heat to maintain the pressure. Cook for 20 minutes. Remove from the heat and quick-release the pressure. Open the lid, tilting it away from you to block any escaping steam. Switch the positions of the ribs from top to bottom. Cover again, bring to high pressure, and cook for an additional 20 minutes.

4. Meanwhile, preheat the oven to 400°F. Line a baking sheet with aluminum foil and spray with the cooking oil.

5. Remove the pot from the heat and quick-release the pressure. Open the lid, tilting it away from you to block any escaping steam. Transfer the short ribs to a wire rack set over a jelly-roll pan and let drain. Pat the ribs dry with paper towels. (The ribs can be prepared up to this point 1 hour ahead and stored, loosely covered with aluminum foil, at room temperature. If desired, strain the cooking liquid and cool to room

temperature. Refrigerate overnight, and remove the hardened fat on the surface. Use as beef broth.)

6. To make the deviled crust: In a small bowl, mix the mustard, garlic, and hot pepper. Mix the bread crumbs and olive oil in a shallow dish until the crumbs are evenly moistened. Brush the meaty part of the ribs with the mustard mixture and roll in the bread crumbs. Place on the prepared baking sheet. Bake, turning once, until the crust is lightly browned, 10 to 15 minutes. Serve hot.

Makes 4 servings
Two 20-minute periods

beef brisket with onion-raisin sauce

L ong-cooked beef brisket is a real treat, but it can take hours. Until the pressure cooker came into our lives, we cooked it only occasionally. Now it offers one of the easiest ways to get dinner on the table, and in much less time. Try this as a sandwich—thinly slice the brisket and serve it on soft buns, with the onion-raisin sauce spooned on top.

1 tablespoon vegetable oil
3 medium onions, cut into ½-inch-wide half-moons
4 medium carrots, cut into ½-inch rounds
½ cup raisins
½ cup Homemade Beef Stock (page 24) or canned low-sodium beef broth (see Note)
2 tablespoons cider vinegar
2 tablespoons light brown sugar
1 bay leaf
One 3-pound first-cut beef brisket, trimmed
½ teaspoon salt
½ teaspoon freshly ground black pepper

1. In a 5- to 7-quart pressure cooker, heat the oil over medium heat. Add the onions and carrots and cook until the vegetables begin to soften, about 2 minutes. Stir in the raisins, stock, vinegar, brown sugar, and bay leaf. Season the brisket with the salt and pepper. Place the brisket in the pot (it may touch the sides, but that's fine).

2. Lock the lid in place. Bring to high pressure over high heat. Adjust the heat to maintain high pressure. Cook for 1 hour. Let the steam release naturally (allow about 15 minutes). Open the lid, tilting it away from you to block any escaping steam.

3. Transfer the brisket to a serving platter and cover with foil to keep warm. Skim any fat from the surface of the cooking liquid. Bring to a boil over high heat. Cook, uncovered, until the liquid is reduced by about half, about 5 minutes. Discard the bay leaf. Pour the sauce into a bowl.

4. Thinly slice the brisket across the grain. Serve with the onion-raisin sauce.

Note: If needed, add more stock to meet your cooker's minimum liquid requirement. Boil the cooking liquid as needed to reduce to sauce consistency.

Makes 4 to 6 servings
1 hour at high pressure

M E A T   M A I N   C O U R S E S

sweet-and-spicy **barbecued** country **ribs**

This is the recipe to make when you hanker for finger-licking ribs, but you don't want to crank up the outdoor grill. Our two-step pressure-cook-and-glaze procedure ensures great results. We prefer meaty country ribs to spareribs for this recipe. Serve it with cornbread and coleslaw for a delicious down-home meal.

1 tablespoon vegetable oil
3 pounds country pork ribs, cut into individual ribs (8 ribs)
½ teaspoon salt
¼ teaspoon freshly ground black pepper
1 medium onion, chopped
2 garlic cloves, minced
1 cup catsup
½ cup jalapeño jelly or apricot preserves
2 teaspoons chili powder
½ cup water

1. In a 5- to 7-quart pressure cooker, heat the oil over medium-high heat. In batches, add the ribs and brown lightly, about 5 minutes. Transfer to a plate, season with the salt and pepper, and set aside.

2. Pour out all but 1 tablespoon of the fat in the pot. Add the onion and garlic and cook until barely softened, about 1 minute. Stir in the catsup, jelly, chili powder, and water. Return the ribs to the pot.

3. Lock the lid in place. Bring to high pressure over high heat. Adjust the heat to maintain the pressure. Cook for 25 minutes. Remove from the heat and quick-release the pressure. Open the lid, tilting it away from you to block any escaping steam. Transfer the ribs to a platter and cover with foil to keep warm.

4. Position a rack 6 inches from the source of heat and preheat the broiler. Lightly oil the broiler rack.

5. While the broiler is heating, let the cooking liquid stand for 3 minutes. Skim off the fat that rises to the top. Bring to a boil over high heat. Cook, uncovered, stirring often, until thickened and reduced to about 2 cups, about 12 minutes.

6. Arrange the ribs on the prepared broiler rack. Brush with some sauce. Broil until glazed, about 2 minutes. Turn, brush with more sauce, and broil until the other side is glazed, about 2 minutes. Serve immediately, with the remaining sauce on the side.

Makes 4 servings
25 minutes at high pressure

pork chops with cherry—black currant sauce

Arlene adapted this recipe from *The Silver Palate Cookbook*. We've added some brown sugar to balance the tart flavors (add it to taste, because the sweetness varies with each brand of currant preserves) and some dried cherries for texture. When choosing pork loin chops for the pressure cooker, ask for the ones closer to the rib section. They will be slightly less lean and with more muscle separations, but they will not dry out as easily as center-cut chops. The timing is very precise, so have the timer set and ready to activate as soon as the pot reaches pressure.

¼ cup dried cherries or cranberries
1 tablespoon vegetable oil
Six 8-ounce pork loin chops, cut 1 inch thick
   from the rib end, well trimmed of excess fat
¼ teaspoon salt, plus more to taste
⅛ teaspoon freshly ground black pepper, plus
   more to taste
¼ cup high-quality black currant preserves
1½ tablespoons Dijon mustard
⅓ cup white wine vinegar
2 tablespoons light brown sugar

1. Preheat the oven to 200°F. In a small bowl, soak the dried cherries or cranberries in warm water to cover until plumped, about 10 minutes. Drain.

2. In a 5- to 7-quart pressure cooker, heat the oil over medium-high heat. Lightly season the pork chops with ¼ teaspoon salt and ⅛ teaspoon pepper. In batches, place in the pot and cook, turning once, until browned on both sides, about 3 minutes. Transfer to a plate.

3. Meanwhile, in a small bowl, mix the preserves and mustard. Return the chops to the pot, slathering the top of each one with the preserve mixture. Lock the lid in place. Bring to high pressure over high heat. Adjust the heat to maintain the temperature. Cook for 1 minute, 15 seconds. Remove from the heat and quick-release the pressure. Open the lid, tilting it away from you to block any escaping steam. Transfer the pork chops to a platter, cover loosely with foil, and keep warm in the oven while making the sauce.

4. Using a wooden spoon, stir the vinegar and brown sugar into the pot, scraping up any browned bits from the bottom and sides of the pan. Cook, uncovered, until the sauce is thickened and reduced by about half, 3 to 5 minutes. Pour any juices from the chops into the sauce and boil for a few seconds. Season with additional salt and pepper. Pour the sauce over the pork chops and serve immediately.

Makes 4 servings
1 minute, 15 seconds at high pressure

pork and winter squash stew with sage

The success of this autumnal stew depends on the cut of pork. Boneless pork shoulder cubes are sometimes available at the butcher, but it's more reliable to cut up your own roast. Whole pork shoulders (also called *pernil* or *calas* at Latino markets) are inexpensive, because there is a fair amount of loss from trimming the fat and skin—a 5-pound shoulder will yield about 2½ pounds of meat after trimming. Even so, pork shoulders are good buys. Serve with bulgur, the nutty flavor of which is the perfect foil for this stew.

2 tablespoons vegetable oil
2½ pounds boneless pork shoulder, cut into 1½-inch cubes
½ teaspoon salt, plus more to taste
¼ teaspoon freshly ground black pepper, plus more to taste
4 medium carrots, cut into 1-inch lengths
1 cup chopped leeks, white and pale green parts only
1 medium red bell pepper, seeded and chopped
2 garlic cloves, minced
⅓ cup dry sherry
1 tablespoon red wine vinegar
1½ cups Homemade Chicken Stock (page 23) or canned low-sodium broth
One medium (1¾ pounds) butternut squash, peeled, seeded, and cut into 1-inch cubes
2 tablespoons cold water
1½ tablespoons cornstarch
1 tablespoon chopped fresh sage

1. In a 5- to 7-quart pressure cooker, heat 1 tablespoon of the oil over medium-high heat. In batches, add the pork and cook, turning occasionally, until lightly browned, about 4 minutes. Transfer to a plate, season with ½ teaspoon salt and ¼ teaspoon pepper, and set aside.

2. Add the remaining 1 tablespoon oil to the pot and return to medium heat. Add the carrots, leeks, red pepper, and garlic. Cook, stirring often, until the vegetables begin to soften, about 2 minutes. Add the sherry and vinegar and stir, scraping up the browned bits on the bottom of the pot with a wooden spoon. Stir in the stock. Return the pork and any juices on the plate to the pot.

3. Lock the lid in place. Bring to high pressure over high heat. Adjust the heat to maintain the pressure. Cook for 25 minutes. Remove from the heat and quick-release the pressure. Open the lid, tilting it away from you to block any escaping steam. Add the squash. Lock the lid in place again and bring to high pressure over high heat. Cook for 1 minute. Remove from the heat and quick-release the pressure. Open the lid. Using a large skimmer or slotted spoon, transfer the meat and vegetables to a serving bowl.

4. Skim any fat from the surface of the cooking liquid. Return the cooker to medium heat and bring the liquid to a simmer. Place the water in a small bowl, sprinkle with the cornstarch, and stir to dissolve. Stir into the simmering liquid and cook until thickened. Stir in the sage. Season with additional salt and pepper. Pour the sauce over the stew, and serve hot.

Makes 6 servings
25 minutes at high pressure for the pork,
then 1 minute at high pressure for the squash

five-spice pork roast

This Asian-inspired roast is rubbed with five-spice powder (available at Asian grocers and many supermarkets) and cooked in a ginger-scented broth. Steam asparagus spears to serve on the side, along with rice to soak up the delicious sauce.

1 tablespoon vegetable oil
One 3-pound boneless center-cut pork loin, fat trimmed to ⅛ inch, tied
½ teaspoon five-spice powder
¼ teaspoon salt
1 scallion, white and green parts, coarsely chopped
2 tablespoons shredded fresh ginger (use the large holes on a box grater)
1 garlic clove, crushed under a knife and peeled
2 tablespoons dry sherry
1 cup Homemade Chicken Stock (page 23) or canned low-sodium broth
2 tablespoons Japanese soy sauce
1½ tablespoons cornstarch
Freshly ground black pepper, to taste
Chopped scallion greens, for garnish

1. In a 5- to 7-quart pressure cooker over medium-high heat, heat the oil. Add the pork roast and cook, turning occasionally, until lightly browned on all sides, about 4 minutes. Transfer the pork to a platter. In a small bowl, mix the five-spice powder and salt together, and season the pork with the mixture.

2. Add the scallion, ginger, and garlic to the pot. Stir over medium heat until fragrant, about 30 seconds. Add the sherry and stir well. Add the stock, stirring to scrape up the browned bits on the bottom of the pot with a wooden spoon. Return the pork to the pot.

3. Lock the lid in place. Bring to high pressure over high heat. Adjust the heat to maintain the pressure. Cook for 30 minutes. Remove from the heat and quick-release the pressure. Open the lid, tilting it away from you to block any escaping steam. Insert a meat thermometer in the center of the roast. It should read about 150°F. The temperature of the roast will rise another 5° to 10°F while standing. Transfer the roast to a serving platter and cover loosely with aluminum foil. Let the roast stand for 10 minutes before carving.

4. Let the cooking liquid stand for 5 minutes. Skim off any fat that rises to the surface. Return the cooking liquid to medium heat and bring to a boil, uncovered. Place the soy sauce in a small bowl, sprinkle with the cornstarch, and stir to dissolve. Stir into the boiling liquid and cook until thickened. Season the sauce with pepper.

5. Remove the strings and slice the roast. Arrange the roast on the platter and sprinkle with the scallions. Serve immediately, with the sauce passed on the side.

Makes 6 servings
30 minutes at high pressure

veal roast with prosciutto, sage, and lemon

Veal shoulder is a succulent cut of meat and one that takes especially well to pressure-cooking. A symbiotic trio of prosciutto, fresh sage, and lemon juice make this a delicious pot roast with only a few tablespoons of sauce, but that sauce will be packed with flavor. Tell the delicatessen counter not to slice the prosciutto too thin—it should not be paper-thin, or you won't be able to taste it. And don't trim off the prosciutto fat! It will melt into the lean veal and baste it from the inside.

One 2-pound veal shoulder roast
2 ounces sliced prosciutto
3 teaspoons chopped fresh sage
¼ teaspoon salt, plus more to taste
⅛ teaspoon freshly ground black pepper, plus
    more to taste
1 tablespoon olive oil
1 garlic clove, finely chopped
½ cup dry white wine, such as Pinot Grigio or
    Sauvignon Blanc
½ cup water
1 tablespoon fresh lemon juice, plus more to taste

1. Untie the roast and unroll it. Place the prosciutto over the surface of the veal, trimming the prosciutto to fit. Sprinkle with 1 teaspoon sage. Roll the roast up and tie crosswise with kitchen string at 2-inch intervals. Season with ¼ teaspoon salt and ⅛ teaspoon pepper.

2. In a 5- to 7-quart pressure cooker, heat the oil over medium-high heat. Add the veal and cook, turning occasionally, until lightly browned on all sides, about 4 minutes. Transfer the veal to a plate.

3. Add the garlic to the cooker and stir until fragrant, about 30 seconds. Do not brown. Add the wine and stir to release the browned bits on the bottom of the cooker. Stir in the water. Return the veal to the cooker.

4. Lock the lid in place. Bring to high pressure over high heat. Adjust the heat to maintain the pressure. Cook for 40 minutes. Remove from the heat and quick-release the pressure. Open the lid, tilting it away from you to block any escaping steam. Transfer the veal to a serving platter and cover loosely with foil to keep warm.

5. Skim any fat from the surface of the cooking liquid. Add the lemon juice and remaining 2 teaspoons sage. Bring to a boil over high heat. Boil, uncovered, until the liquid is thickened and evaporated by about half, about 6 minutes. Season with additional lemon juice, salt, and pepper.

6. Remove the string and carve the veal crosswise into thick slices. Serve, spooning the sauce over the veal.

Makes 6 servings
40 minutes at high pressure

osso bucco presto

One day while testing recipes for this book, Rick's friend Kelly Volpe was in the kitchen helping out. Rick served her a bowl of this tender, fragrant osso bucco, and for the rest of the afternoon, Kelly kept muttering, "I can't believe that osso bucco cooked for only 25 minutes!" These veal shanks are so good that you may find they don't even need the gremolata finish. Unfortunately, cross-cut veal shanks for osso bucco have become pricey, so you may have to save this recipe for company, or for payday. Choose the meatiest shanks—sometimes you get too much bone. The marrow is delectable, and should be spread onto bread and savored.

2 tablespoons olive oil
6 meaty veal shanks (3¼ pounds), cross-cut 1½ inches thick, tied with kitchen twine (see Note)
½ teaspoon salt
¼ teaspoon freshly ground black pepper
1 medium onion, chopped
1 medium carrot, cut into ½-inch dice
1 medium celery rib, cut into ½-inch dice
2 garlic cloves, minced
½ cup dry white wine
One 15-ounce can tomatoes in juice, drained and chopped, ½ cup tomato juice reserved
½ teaspoon dried basil
½ teaspoon dried rosemary

GREMOLATA
2 tablespoons chopped fresh parsley
Grated zest of 1 lemon
1 garlic clove, minced

1. In a 5- to 7-quart pressure cooker, heat 1 tablespoon of the oil over medium-high heat. In batches, add the veal shanks and cook, turning occasionally, until lightly browned, about 3 minutes. Transfer the veal to a platter and season with the salt and pepper.

2. Add the remaining 1 tablespoon oil to the pressure cooker and heat. Add the onion, carrot, celery, and garlic and cook, stirring occasionally, until softened, about 3 minutes. Stir in the wine and cook until almost evaporated. Add the tomatoes and the ½ cup tomato juice, basil, and rosemary. Return the veal to the pressure cooker.

3. Lock the lid in place. Bring to high pressure over high heat. Adjust the heat to maintain the pressure. Cook for 25 minutes.

4. Meanwhile, make the gremolata: In a small bowl, combine the parsley, lemon zest, and garlic. Set aside.

5. Remove the cooker from the heat and quick-release the pressure. Open the lid, tilting it away from you to block any escaping steam. Arrange the veal on a serving platter. Pour the tomato sauce over the veal. Sprinkle with the gremolata and serve immediately.

Note: If the butcher hasn't already done so, tie the shanks with kitchen twine to hold the meat in shape during cooking. Tie each piece of veal securely around its circumference. To hold the marrow in place, tie again over the top of the bone.

Makes 4 servings
25 minutes at high pressure

veal breast with white wine and herbs

Veal breast is beloved by European cooks, who prize its gelatinous, flavorful meat. It must be long-cooked to transform it from a tough piece of meat into one of the most tender, melt-in-your-mouth dishes around, and pressure cooking does this better and more quickly than any other method. Veal breast is sometimes boned and stuffed, but try it this way—unstuffed, with classic flavors of white wine, shallots, and herbs. It is wonderful served with oven-roasted potatoes.

2 tablespoons extra-virgin olive oil
One 4-pound, 3-rib veal breast (see Note), trimmed
¼ teaspoon salt, plus more to taste
¼ teaspoon freshly ground black pepper, plus more to taste
¼ cup finely chopped shallot
1 garlic clove, minced
¼ cup dry white wine
½ cup Homemade Veal or Chicken Stock (pages 24 and 23) or canned low-sodium broth
¾ teaspoon dried thyme
¾ teaspoon dried rosemary

1. In a 5- to 7-quart pressure cooker, heat the oil over medium-high heat. Season the veal breast with ¼ teaspoon salt and ¼ teaspoon pepper. Place in the pot and brown on both sides, about 5 minutes. Transfer to a plate.

2. Add the shallot and garlic to the pot and cook, stirring often, until softened, about 1 minute. Add the wine and cook until almost completely reduced, about 1 minute. Stir in the stock. Return the veal breast to the pot, and sprinkle with the thyme and rosemary.

3. Lock the lid in place. Bring to high pressure over high heat. Adjust the heat to maintain the pressure. Cook for 1 hour. Remove from the heat and quick-release the pressure. Open the lid, tilting it away from you to block any escaping steam. Transfer the veal to a platter and cover with foil to keep warm.

4. Let the cooking liquid stand for 5 minutes. Skim off any fat from the surface. Bring to a boil, uncovered, over high heat. Cook, uncovered, until slightly reduced, about 5 minutes. Season the sauce with additional salt and pepper. Pour the sauce into a sauceboat.

5. Carve the veal breast and serve with the sauce passed on the side.

Note: Ask the butcher to cut the breast bones horizontally about 3 inches from the bottom of the roast (at the thin end), cutting just through the bones to the meat to create a "hinged" piece of meat and bone. The breast can now be folded at the hinge to fit into a 5- to 7-quart pressure cooker. (You may not have to ask the butcher to do this—in some Italian neighborhoods, it is done as a matter of course.)

Makes 3 to 4 servings
1 hour at high pressure

poultry and seafood

No matter what method is used to prepare them, poultry and seafood should never be overcooked— and it takes a little special attention to avoid this problem in the pressure cooker. The cooking times may seem ridiculously short, but resist the temptation to add extra time until you stop the cooking and check for doneness.

Poultry remains one of America's most popular foods. When preparing chicken or turkey in a pressure cooker, we prefer to remove the skin. The main reason is aesthetic (the skin shrivels unattractively), but there are health benefits, too, as it greatly reduces the amount of fat in the dish. Almost every cook knows that there is a lot of fat lurking in the skin of chicken and turkey. Remove the poultry skin, and there goes one-third of the fat grams. When poultry with its skin is cooked in a pressure cooker, the skin releases so much fat into the cooking liquid that it is difficult to skim off the fat from the liquid before serving. Of course, it's almost impossible to take the skin off chicken wings, so we always remove them when cutting up a chicken.

Seafood, including fish and shellfish (except for some squid recipes), has relatively short cooking times. We usually grill or sauté our seafood in minutes, and we don't see much good in searching for ways to cook it in the pressure cooker. But there are times when a soothing, flavorful seafood stew really fills the bill. In that case, we press the pressure cooker into service to prepare a tasty base mixture, and add the seafood at the last minute, just to cook through.

tips for poultry and seafood

➤ Before cooking poultry, always remove as much skin as possible. In most dishes, skinned chicken on the bone will give the best results. But, if cooked properly, boneless skinless chicken, even breast meat, will be perfectly succulent in the pressure cooker.

➤ If the recipe calls for a whole chicken, it should be cut up into quarters (with the wings removed) to fit into the pot. A 4-pound chicken is the perfect weight to give good-sized portions that cook in 10 minutes. Depending on the appetites at the table, a 4-pound chicken will serve two to four people.

➤ Instead of buying chicken quarters, cut up the chicken yourself. This will give you the back portion, neck, giblets, and wings to turn into stock. Store the pieces in the freezer until you have enough to make a batch.

To cut a chicken into quarters, use a large sharp knife. Set aside the neck and giblets. Make a slit down the backbone—this loosens the skin and makes it easier to cut up the chicken. Cut off the wings at the shoulder joints. On one side of the chicken, make an incision in the skin near the hip joint to reveal the joint. Pull one leg quarter away from the body so the joint pops out of the socket, and cut off the leg quarter at the joint. Repeat with the other leg quarter to give you two leg/drumstick quarters.

Fold the back away from the body to break it, and cut off the back portion at the break. Cut down one side of the backbone on the carcass. Cut through the keel bone (the thin, flexible, cartilage-like bone that separates the two breast halves) to divide the breast in half lengthwise. The backbone will still be attached to one breast half; cut it off lengthwise. You will have two breasts and two leg quarters, and the back, backbone, neck, giblets, and wings for making stock or another use. Holding the skin with a paper towel, pull it off each breast. Repeat with the leg quarters, starting at the large end of the leg, pulling towards the drumstick, and cutting at the knee (don't worry about the little bit of skin left). Discard the skin.

Dark meat usually takes a bit longer to cook than white meat. Put the leg quarters in the cooker first, then the breasts. The legs in the cooking liquid will get a little extra cooking time as the liquid comes to a boil.

➤ Buy your fish on the bone, and ask the fish-monger to fillet them for you. Take home the bones and head to make Homemade Fish Stock (page 25).

➤ Homemade Fish Stock is delicious, but you can substitute bottled clam juice, if you like. Dilute the clam juice with equal portions of water, or it could be too salty in the pressure cooker.

hunter's-style chicken

What we call chicken cacciatore, the Italians call *pollo alla cacciatorra,* or hunter's-style chicken, because a hunter would bring home wild mushrooms from the forest along with whatever else he may have bagged. A good way to serve this earthy dish is on a bed of orzo pasta.

½ cup (½ ounce) dried porcini mushrooms
1 tablespoon olive oil
8 ounces fresh white mushrooms, thinly sliced
1 medium onion, chopped
2 medium celery ribs, cut into ¼-inch-thick pieces
1 medium red bell pepper, seeded and chopped
1 garlic clove, finely chopped
½ cup hearty red wine, such as Zinfandel
One 14½-ounce can tomatoes in juice, drained and chopped
½ cup water
¾ teaspoon Italian seasoning, or ¼ teaspoon each dried rosemary, basil, and sage
¼ teaspoon crushed hot red pepper flakes
One 4-pound chicken, quartered, skin removed (see page 74)
¼ teaspoon salt

1. Rinse the dried mushrooms under cold running water to remove any grit. Set aside.

2. In a 5- to 7-quart pressure cooker, heat the oil over medium-high heat. Add the fresh and dried mushrooms, onion, celery, sweet red pepper, and garlic. Cook until the mushrooms begin to soften, about 3 minutes. Add the red wine and bring to a boil. Stir in the tomatoes, water, Italian seasonings, and crushed red pepper. Season the chicken with the salt. Place in the cooker, leg quarters first, then the breasts, meaty sides up.

3. Lock the lid in place. Bring to high pressure over high heat. Adjust the heat to maintain the pressure. Cook for 10 minutes. Remove from the heat and quick-release the pressure. Open the lid, tilting it away from you to block any escaping steam. Transfer the chicken and sauce to a platter and serve immediately.

Makes 2 to 4 servings
10 minutes at high pressure

moroccan chicken with lemon and green olives

The exotic flavors of Moroccan cooking are just the thing to perk up a weeknight chicken supper. Use plump, full-flavored green olives from the delicatessen counter or a high-quality bottled variety. Couscous is the perfect partner for this dish.

½ teaspoon ground cumin
½ teaspoon ground ginger
½ teaspoon ground coriander
½ teaspoon salt
¼ teaspoon crushed hot red pepper flakes
One 4-pound chicken, quartered, skin removed (see page 74)
1 tablespoon olive oil
1 small onion, finely chopped
3 garlic cloves, finely chopped
1 cup Homemade Chicken Stock (page 23) or canned low-sodium broth
¼ cup fresh lemon juice
6 ounces Mediterranean green olives, pitted and coarsely chopped
2 tablespoons chopped fresh cilantro

1. In a small bowl, mix the cumin, ginger, coriander, salt, and red pepper. Rub the mixture all over the chicken. Set aside for 10 minutes.

2. In a 5- to 7-quart pressure cooker, heat the oil over medium-high heat. In batches, cook the chicken, turning once, until lightly browned on both sides, about 3 minutes. Transfer to a plate and set aside.

3. Add the onion and garlic and cook until the onion begins to soften, about 1 minute. Stir in the stock. Return the chicken to the cooker, leg quarters first, then the breast, meaty sides up. Lock the lid in place. Bring to high pressure over high heat. Adjust the heat to maintain the pressure. Cook for 10 minutes. Remove from the heat and quick-release the pressure. Open the lid, tilting it away from you to block any escaping steam. Transfer the chicken to a serving platter and cover with aluminum foil to keep warm.

4. Skim any fat from the surface of the cooking liquid. Stir the lemon juice and olives into the cooking liquid. Bring to a boil, uncovered, over medium-high heat. Cook until slightly thickened, about 5 minutes. Pour over the chicken and sprinkle with the cilantro. Serve hot.

Makes 2 to 4 servings
10 minutes at high pressure

bbq chicken

Arlene says that she remembers her mother making barbecue chicken in her pressure cooker during the pot's first big splash in the American kitchen in the forties and fifties. The old way had just two ingredients, chicken and bottled barbecue sauce. This recipe gives you an opportunity to use your favorite sauce, but most of them tend to scorch. Sidestep this problem by adding some water to the sauce. A quick glaze under the broiler gives a delectable finish. To complete the meal, serve with home-fried potatoes and a crisp salad.

1 tablespoon vegetable oil
1 medium onion, chopped
2 garlic cloves, chopped
½ cup prepared barbecue sauce
½ cup water
One 4-pound chicken, quartered, with skin removed (see page 74)
¼ teaspoon salt
⅛ teaspoon freshly ground black pepper

1. In a 5- to 7-quart pressure cooker, heat the oil over medium heat. Add the onion and garlic and cook until the vegetables soften, about 2 minutes. Stir in the barbecue sauce and water. Add the chicken, leg quarters first, then the breasts, meaty sides up.

2. Lock the lid in place. Bring to high pressure over high heat. Adjust the heat to maintain the pressure. Cook for 10 minutes. Quick-release the pressure. Open the lid, tilting it away from you to block any escaping steam. (Don't worry if the chicken looks a little pink at the bone, as it will continue to cook in the broiler.) Transfer the chicken to an oiled broiler rack. Season the chicken with the salt and pepper and set aside.

3. Position the broiler pan 6 inches from the source of heat and preheat the broiler. Meanwhile, bring the cooking liquid in the pot to a boil over medium-high heat. Cook uncovered, stirring often to avoid scorching, until the sauce thickens, about 5 minutes.

4. Brush the chicken with the sauce. Broil until glazed, 2 to 3 minutes. Turn, brush with additional sauce, and broil until the other side is glazed. Serve hot, with the additional sauce on the side.

Makes 2 to 4 servings
10 minutes at high pressure

mexican chicken in soft tacos

Here's a mildly spiced chicken, onion, and peppers mixture to roll up in warm tortillas for a very quick meal. You may use your favorite bottled salsa, but why not make fresh salsa while the chicken cooks? It will take only a few minutes, and the chunkiness of homemade salsa is a nice contrast to the meltingly tender chicken. If you have a few extra minutes, boil the cooking liquid down and stir into the chicken and vegetables—though not essential, it will give a bit of extra flavor.

1 tablespoon olive oil
1 medium onion, cut into ½-inch-thick half-moons
1 medium red bell pepper, seeded and cut into ½-inch-thick strips
1 jalapeño chile, seeded and minced
1 garlic clove, minced
½ teaspoon dried oregano
½ teaspoon ground cumin
½ cup water
6 boneless, skinless chicken thighs
¼ teaspoon salt
¼ teaspoon freshly ground black pepper
3 tablespoons chopped fresh cilantro (optional)

SALSA
8 ripe plum tomatoes, seeded and chopped into ½-inch dice (pulse in a food processor, if desired)
1 ripe avocado, pit removed, peeled, and chopped (optional)
2 tablespoons finely chopped onion
1 tablespoon fresh lime juice
1 jalapeño chile, seeded and minced
1 garlic clove, crushed through a press
¼ teaspoon salt

8 warmed flour tortillas, for serving

1. In a 5- to 7-quart pressure cooker, heat the oil over medium-high heat. Add the onion, red pepper, jalapeño, garlic, oregano, and cumin. Cook, stirring often, until the onion begins to soften, about 2 minutes. Stir in the water. Season the chicken with the salt and pepper. Add to the pot. Lock the lid in place. Bring to high pressure over high heat. Adjust the heat to maintain the pressure. Cook for 7 minutes.

2. Meanwhile, make the salsa: In a medium bowl, mix all of the ingredients and set aside at room temperature.

3. Remove the pressure cooker from the heat and quick-release the pressure. Open the lid, tilting it away from you to block any escaping steam. Transfer the chicken to a cutting board. Using a large knife, coarsely chop the chicken and transfer to a serving bowl. Using a slotted spoon, transfer the vegetables to the bowl. Stir in the cilantro, if desired. Cover with aluminum foil to keep warm.

4. If desired, return the uncovered pot to high heat. Boil the cooking liquid until evaporated to a few tablespoons, about 6 minutes. Stir into the chicken and vegetables.

5. To serve, spoon the chicken-and-vegetable mixture and the salsa into a tortilla, and roll up.

Makes 8 tacos
7 minutes at high pressure

chicken with **tarragon-mustard** sauce

This is a versatile dish that is easy enough for a weeknight meal, but special enough for company. Broccoli is the perfect green vegetable to go with the mustard sauce. Serve with hot cooked egg noodles to soak up every last drop.

½ teaspoon dried tarragon
½ teaspoon salt, plus more to taste
¼ teaspoon freshly ground black pepper, plus more to taste
One 4-pound chicken, quartered and skinned (see page 74)
1 tablespoon vegetable oil
1 tablespoon unsalted butter
⅓ cup chopped shallots
½ cup dry white wine
½ cup Homemade Chicken Stock (page 23), or use canned low-sodium broth
2 tablespoons heavy cream
1 tablespoon Dijon mustard
1 tablespoon cornstarch
2 tablespoons chopped fresh parsley, for garnish

1. In a small bowl, rub the tarragon, ½ teaspoon salt, and ¼ teaspoon pepper together with your fingertips to crumble the tarragon well. Sprinkle the mixture all over the chicken.

2. In a 5- to 7-quart pressure cooker, heat the oil over medium-high heat. In batches, cook the chicken, turning once, until lightly browned on both sides, about 3 minutes. Transfer to a plate and set aside.

3. Pour out any oil in the cooker. Add the butter and heat over medium heat. Add the shallots and stir until softened, about 1 minute. Add the wine and bring to a boil, scraping up any browned bits on the bottom of the cooker. Stir in the stock.

4. Return the chicken to the cooker, leg quarters first, then the breast, meaty sides up. Lock the lid in place. Bring to high pressure over high heat. Adjust the heat to maintain the pressure. Cook for 10 minutes. Remove from the heat and quick-release the pressure. Open the lid, tilting it away from you to block any escaping steam. Transfer the chicken to a serving platter and cover with aluminum foil to keep warm.

5. Skim any fat from the surface of the cooking liquid. Bring to a boil, uncovered, over medium heat. In a small bowl, combine the cream and mustard. Add the cornstarch and stir until it is completely dissolved. Stir into the boiling liquid and cook just until thickened. Season the sauce with additional salt and pepper. Pour over the chicken, sprinkle with parsley, and serve immediately.

Makes 2 to 4 servings
10 minutes at high pressure

turkey breast with marsala and mushrooms

Tender turkey breast is a wonderful ingredient. Its neutral flavor is complemented by many different flavors. Here, dry Marsala wine, mushrooms, and a touch of cream make a luxurious sauce, perfect for spooning over rice.

Two (1¼ pounds each) boneless, skinless turkey breast roasts (see Note)
¼ teaspoon salt, plus more to taste
¼ teaspoon freshly ground black pepper, plus more to taste
2 tablespoons olive oil
6 ounces fresh white mushrooms, thinly sliced
3 tablespoons chopped shallots
1 garlic clove, minced
½ teaspoon dried thyme
⅔ cup Homemade Chicken Stock (page 23) or canned low-sodium broth
⅓ cup dry Marsala
1½ tablespoons cornstarch
3 tablespoons heavy cream

1. Working with one roast at a time, locate the silver-colored sinew that runs the length of the roast. Hold the tip of the sinew and use a sharp knife to scrape it away from the meat. Trim any fat from the roast. Tie the roast crosswise at 2-inch intervals with kitchen string. Repeat with the other roast. Season the breasts with ¼ teaspoon salt and ¼ teaspoon pepper.

2. In a 5- to 7-quart pressure cooker, heat 1 tablespoon of the oil over medium-high heat. Add the breasts and cook, turning occasionally, until lightly browned, about 3 minutes. Transfer to a plate and set aside.

3. Add the remaining 1 tablespoon oil to the cooker and heat. Add the mushrooms, shallots, gar-

lic, and thyme. Cook until the mushrooms begin to soften, about 3 minutes. Return the roasts to the cooker and add the stock and the Marsala.

4. Lock the lid in place. Bring to high pressure over high heat. Adjust the heat to maintain the pressure. Cook for 15 minutes. Remove from the heat and quick-release the pressure. Check the turkey for doneness: An instant-read thermometer inserted in the center of the roasts should read 160°F or above. Transfer the roasts to a carving platter and cover loosely with foil to keep warm.

5. Return the uncovered cooker to high heat and bring the cooking liquid to a boil. In a small bowl, sprinkle the cornstarch over the heavy cream and whisk until smooth. Whisk the cream mixture into the boiling liquid and cook until thickened. Season with additional salt and pepper. Transfer the sauce to a warmed bowl.

6. Remove the strings from the roasts. Using a sharp knife, cut the turkey into ½-inch-thick slices. Serve immediately, passing the sauce on the side.

Note: Many supermarkets carry boneless, skinless turkey breasts, but whole turkey breasts are much more common. To get two 1¼-pound boneless breast roasts, purchase a 5½-pound whole breast. To bone out the breasts, pull off the skin. Using the tip of a sharp knife, starting at the breast bone, cut down one side of the rib cage, removing one half of the breast meat in one piece. Repeat with the other side.

Makes 6 to 8 servings
15 minutes at high pressure

north beach **cioppino**

In San Francisco's North Beach, this fragrant fish stew is served at every kind of restaurant, from countertop luncheonette to formal bastion of *la cucina Italiana*. (Portuguese and Italian fishermen hotly dispute the origin of cioppino, but because Italian immigrants own more restaurants than the Portuguese, they seem to have won the argument.) It is often made with cracked Dungeness crab, and even though it's delicious, the crab shells make the dish somewhat difficult to eat politely. Stir in shelled crabmeat just before serving—the hot broth will heat it through.

2 tablespoons olive oil
1 medium onion, chopped
1 medium red or green bell pepper, seeded and chopped
2 celery ribs with leaves, chopped
2 garlic cloves, finely chopped
½ cup hearty red wine, such as Zinfandel
2 cups Homemade Fish Stock (page 25) or 1 cup bottled clam juice and 1 cup water
One 28-ounce can tomatoes in juice, drained and chopped
2 tablespoons tomato paste
½ teaspoon dried oregano
½ teaspoon dried basil
1 bay leaf
¼ teaspoon salt
¼ teaspoon crushed hot red pepper flakes
12 ounces skinless cod fillet, cut into 1-inch pieces
8 ounces medium shrimp, peeled and deveined
8 ounces lump crabmeat, picked over for cartilage

1. In a 5- to 7-quart pressure cooker, heat the oil over medium-high heat. Add the onion, red or green pepper, celery, and garlic. Cook, stirring often, until the vegetables begin to soften, about 2 minutes. Add the wine and bring to a boil. Stir in the stock, tomatoes, tomato paste, oregano, basil, bay leaf, salt, and hot pepper.

2. Lock the lid in place. Bring to high pressure over high heat. Adjust the heat to maintain the pressure. Cook for 10 minutes. Remove from the heat and quick-release the pressure. Open the lid, tilting it away from you to block any escaping steam.

3. Return the cooker to medium heat. Bring the cooking liquid to a simmer over medium heat, uncovered. Add the cod and shrimp and simmer until the fish turns opaque, about 2 minutes. Do not overcook. Stir in the crabmeat and remove from the heat.

4. Serve immediately in deep soup bowls.

Makes 8 servings
10 minutes at high pressure

shrimp and sausage gumbo

S ome folks might consider gumbo a rib-sticking soup. As it is certainly substantial enough to make a meal, we think of it as a light stew, and one that we make often for supper. This basic recipe is very versatile, and can be turned into chicken or fish gumbo with a few simple substitutions. One of the essential ingredients of gumbo is roux, traditionally a browned combination of fat and flour. By toasting the flour alone in a skillet, you'll get the flavor without the extra fat. Another must-have is okra, whose juices help thicken the gumbo. If you don't like okra, you can leave it out or substitute green beans, but the gumbo won't be as thick.

1 tablespoon oil
8 ounces andouille or other smoked sausage, such as kielbasa, cut into ¼-inch-thick rounds
1 medium onion, chopped
1 medium celery rib with leaves, chopped
1 medium red bell pepper, seeded and chopped
2 garlic cloves, finely chopped
2 teaspoons Cajun Seasoning (recipe follows)
1 bay leaf
½ teaspoon salt, plus more to taste
4 cups Homemade Chicken Stock (page 23) or canned low-sodium broth
One 14½-ounce can tomatoes in juice, drained and chopped, juices reserved
⅓ cup all-purpose flour
One 10-ounce box frozen okra
1 pound medium shrimp, peeled, deveined, and each cut lengthwise in half
2 cups long-grain rice, cooked according to package directions (about 4 cups cooked rice)

1. In a 5- to 7-quart pressure cooker, heat the oil over medium heat. Add the sausage and cook, stirring often, until lightly browned, about 5 minutes. Stir in the onion, celery, red pepper, and garlic. Cook, stirring occasionally, until the vegetables begin to soften, about 2 minutes. Stir in the Cajun Seasoning, bay leaf, and ½ teaspoon salt. Add the stock, tomatoes, and their juices.

2. Lock the lid in place. Bring to high pressure over high heat. Adjust the heat to maintain pressure. Cook for 8 minutes.

3. Meanwhile, in a medium nonstick skillet over medium heat, cook the flour, stirring often, until it is toasted and turns beige, about 5 minutes. Transfer the toasted flour to a bowl and set aside.

4. Remove the cooker from the heat and quick-release the pressure. Open the lid, tilting it away from you to block any escaping steam. Remove the bay leaf. Gradually whisk about 1¼ cups of the cooking liquid into the flour to make a thin paste. Stir the paste into the cooker. Add the okra. Cook, uncovered, occasionally stirring and breaking up the block of okra, until the okra is tender, about 10 minutes. Stir in the shrimp and cook just until it turns pink and firm, about 1 minute. Season with additional salt.

5. To serve, place a spoonful of hot rice in each bowl. Spoon the gumbo over the rice and serve immediately.

Cajun Seasoning: In a small bowl, combine 2 tablespoons paprika (preferably sweet Hungarian), 1 tablespoon each dried basil and dried thyme, 1 teaspoon each garlic powder and onion powder, ½ tea-

spoon freshly ground black pepper, and ¼ teaspoon
cayenne pepper. Store in a tightly covered jar.

Filé Gumbo: If you wish, use filé powder (ground sas-
safras leaves) to thicken the gumbo. Delete the okra.
Stir the flour mixture into the soup and simmer until
lightly thickened and no trace of raw flour flavor
remains, about 5 minutes. Remove the cooker from
the heat. Gradually stir in enough filé powder to
thicken the gumbo to desired consistency, about 1½
tablespoons. After adding the filé powder, do not
cook the gumbo or freeze it—when simmered, filé
powder makes the gumbo very gooey.

Snapper or Cod Gumbo: Substitute 2 cups bottled clam
juice and 2 cups water for the chicken stock.
Substitute 1½ pounds skinned snapper or cod fillets,
cut into 1-inch cubes, for the shrimp. Simmer until
the fish is opaque, about 3 minutes.

Chicken Gumbo: Delete the shrimp. Brown 1¼ pounds
boneless, skinless chicken thighs to the cooker along
with the sausage. When removing the bay leaf, transfer the chicken thighs to a cutting board and set aside
while the okra is simmering. Cut the chicken into
bite-sized pieces, and return to the gumbo just before
serving.

■■■■■■

Makes 8 to 12 servings
8 minutes at high pressure

normandy **fish chowder** with saffron

This creamy fish chowder can be made with any meaty, firm-fleshed fish such as cod or haddock. If you prefer, substitute shellfish for the fish—the soup is excellent with shrimp, shucked oysters, or a combination.

2 tablespoons unsalted butter
1 cup chopped leeks, white and pale green parts only
2 medium celery ribs with leaves, chopped
1 garlic clove, minced
½ cup dry white wine, such as Sauvignon Blanc
3 cups Homemade Fish Stock (see page 25), or 2 cups bottled clam juice and 1 cup water
¼ teaspoon dried thyme
¼ teaspoon fennel seed
¼ teaspoon salt, plus more to taste
⅛ teaspoon crushed hot red pepper flakes
4 medium (1 pound) red-skinned potatoes, scrubbed, cut into ½-inch dice
⅓ cup heavy cream
¼ teaspoon crumbled saffron threads
2 teaspoons cornstarch
1½ pounds skinless cod or haddock fillets, cut into 1-inch pieces
Chopped fresh parsley, for garnish

1. In a 5- to 7-quart pressure cooker, melt the butter over medium-high heat. Add the leeks, celery, and garlic. Cook, stirring occasionally, until the vegetables begin to soften, about 2 minutes. Add the wine and bring to a boil. Add the stock, thyme, fennel seed, ¼ teaspoon salt, and hot pepper.

2. Lock the lid in place. Bring to high pressure over high heat. Adjust the heat to maintain the pressure. Cook for 10 minutes. Remove from the heat and quick-release the pressure. Open the lid, tilting it away from you to block any escaping steam.

3. Return the cooker to the stove. Add the potatoes to the cooker. Lock the lid in place. Bring to high pressure over high heat and cook for 3 minutes. Quick-release the pressure and open the lid. Reduce the heat to medium.

4. In a small bowl, combine the cream and saffron. Sprinkle the cornstarch into the bowl and mix well to dissolve. Stir into the simmering broth. Add the cod or haddock and cook until the fish is opaque and the liquid is lightly thickened, about 2 minutes. Season with additional salt.

5. Serve immediately in deep soup bowls, sprinkling each serving with parsley.

_____

Makes 6 servings
10 minutes at high pressure for base,
then 3 minutes at high pressure for potatoes

tuna steaks in basque sweet pepper ragout

Piperade, a Basque ragout of meltingly tender sweet peppers with onions, garlic, and tomato, makes a great bed for thick tuna steaks. This is a fine recipe for the pressure-cooker skillet, because it's easiest to get the tuna steaks in and out of a shallow pan. If you are using a 5- to 7-quart cooker, sear the tuna steaks in a separate skillet, then transfer them to the sweet peppers for their brief final cooking. Another option is to separately grill or broil the steaks and serve them atop the ragout. Make some rice or couscous to go alongside, and you'll have a very fast and healthful meal.

2 tablespoons extra-virgin olive oil

Four 6-ounce (1¼ inches thick) tuna steaks

½ teaspoon salt

¼ teaspoon freshly ground black pepper

1 large onion, cut into ¼-inch-thick half-moons

1 medium red bell pepper, seeded and cut into ½-inch-thick strips

1 medium yellow bell pepper, seeded and cut into ½-inch-thick strips

2 garlic cloves, finely chopped

One 14½-ounce can tomatoes in juice, drained and chopped

⅛ teaspoon crushed hot red pepper flakes

⅓ cup Mediterranean black olives, pitted and coarsely chopped

1. In a 2½-quart pressure skillet or a large nonstick skillet, heat 1 tablespoon of the oil over high heat until very hot but not smoking. Season the tuna steaks with ¼ teaspoon salt and the black pepper. Cook, turning once, for 1 minute per side, to just sear the tuna. Transfer to a plate and set aside. Do not cover.

2. In the pressure skillet or a 5- to 7-quart pressure cooker, heat the remaining 1 tablespoon oil over medium heat. Add the onion, red and yellow peppers, and garlic. Cook, stirring often, until the vegetables begin to soften, about 3 minutes. Stir in the tomatoes, the remaining ¼ teaspoon salt, and the hot pepper.

3. Lock the lid in place. Bring to high pressure over high heat. Adjust the heat to maintain the pressure. Cook for 5 minutes. Remove from the heat and quick-release the pressure. Open the lid, tilting it away from you to block any escaping steam.

4. Stir in the olives. Return the tuna to the pressure skillet or cooker. Lock the lid in place and cook over medium heat for 2 minutes—the cooker does not have to return to pressure. The steaks will have an opaque cooked ring surrounding a very rare center; simmer, covered, to cook longer to greater doneness, if desired.

5. Spoon the ragout onto dinner plates and top each serving with a tuna steak. Serve immediately.

Makes 4 servings

5 minutes at high pressure

cheese-stuffed **calamari** in **tomato sauce**

POULTRY AND SEAFOOD

Calamari (call it squid if you like) should be cooked either very quickly or very leisurely — anything in between gives rubbery results. This Sicilian recipe usually needs a laid-back long simmer, but once the calamari are stuffed, the pressure cooker will speed things up considerably. Ask the fish store to pick out its largest cleaned calamari sacks (they're easiest to stuff) and to add a handful of tentacles to the order for the filling, or buy 12 large uncleaned calamari and clean them yourself. There are a couple of different ways to serve the calamari. We serve it in bowls with bread to soak up the extra sauce. Or, serve the calamari on a plate with a spoonful of sauce; toss the remaining sauce with spaghetti and serve it on the side.

SAUCE

- 1 tablespoon olive oil
- 1 medium onion
- 2 garlic cloves, finely chopped
- One 28-ounce can crushed tomatoes
- $1/8$ teaspoon crushed hot red pepper flakes

FILLING

- 4 ounces calamari tentacles, finely chopped
- $2/3$ cup fresh bread crumbs
- $2/3$ cup ricotta cheese
- $1/2$ cup freshly grated Parmesan cheese
- 2 tablespoons chopped fresh basil
- 1 garlic clove, crushed through a press
- $1/8$ teaspoon salt
- $1/8$ teaspoon freshly ground black pepper

- 12 large calamari bodies, cleaned
- Chopped fresh basil, for serving
- Crusty Italian bread, for serving

1. To make the sauce: In a 5- to 7-quart pressure cooker, heat the oil over medium heat. Add the onion and garlic. Cook, stirring often, until the onion begins to soften, about 1 minute. Stir in the tomatoes and hot pepper.

2. Lock the lid in place. Bring to high pressure over high heat. Adjust the heat to maintain the pressure. Cook for 10 minutes. Remove from the heat and quick-release the pressure. Open the lid, tilting it away from you to block any escaping steam.

3. Meanwhile, make the filling: In a medium bowl, combine the chopped calamari tentacles, bread crumbs, ricotta, Parmesan, basil, garlic, salt, and pepper. Loosely stuff the calamari bodies with the filling (your fingers work better than a spoon), leaving some room for expansion, and close the openings with wooden toothpicks. Pinching the openings closed, quickly rinse off any filling on the outsides of the stuffed calamari under gently running cold water.

4. Place the stuffed calamari in the sauce. Lock the lid in place. Return to high pressure over high heat, and adjust the heat to maintain the pressure. Cook for 15 minutes. Remove from the heat and release the pressure by the natural release method.

5. Serve the calamari and sauce in bowls, sprinkled with the basil, and pass the bread on the side.

Makes 4 to 6 servings
10 minutes at high pressure for the sauce,
then 15 minutes at high pressure for the calamari

beans

Beans are being rediscovered for their earthy flavor and healthful profile. The soluble fiber in beans has been linked to lowering blood cholesterol. Combining beans with grains creates a complete protein with all the essential amino acids. (You'll see that most of these recipes are served over rice or some other grain.)

Even in a regular pot, cooking dried beans is never precise. The age and relative dryness of the beans greatly affect the cooking time. Because there are so many variables, cooking charts for the different beans can be frustrating. We think it is best to give yourself a very wide berth when cooking beans to be sure that they don't overcook into mush.

Beans should always be soaked before cooking to help soften the fibers and leach out some of the indigestible enzymes. Many people prefer to soak their beans for at least 4 hours or overnight, which helps the beans keep their shape during cooking.

However, to do this requires thinking ahead. To give more opportunity for spontaneity, the beans can also be quick-soaked in a pressure cooker, then drained and pressure-cooked again for a few minutes. Instead of pressure-cooking the beans until they're tender, you will have more control over the process if you release the pressure and finish cooking them uncovered at normal atmospheric pressure. You'll add only a few minutes' cooking time to the whole procedure, but your beans will be in better shape.

When cooking the beans for a soup or purée, the quest for the perfectly shaped bean isn't a problem. The beans in these dishes can be completely cooked at high pressure. If a few beans are broken up, no one will notice or care. But when you want tender, intact beans for a salad or to stir into a stew, you'll be glad you used the two-step procedure.

tips for **beans**

➤ Old beans take forever to cook. As the freshness of beans is so important, buy them from a source with a high turnover. At a supermarket, Latino brands are a good bet; you can also purchase fresh dried beans at a natural foods store.

➤ To soak dried beans in a bowl, rinse the beans in a sieve, sorting through them to remove any stones. Place in a large bowl. Add enough cold water to cover the beans by at least 2 inches. The ideal soaking time is 4 to 6 hours. After that, the beans can hydrate *too* much, making it difficult to pressure-cook them without their breaking up. (As a matter of convenience, you can soak the beans for up to 12 hours. These long-soaked beans are best for cooking into soups or purées. Some thick-skinned beans, such as soybeans and large lima beans, need overnight soaking to properly soften their skins. Most cookbooks say "overnight," but realistically speaking, you would probably soak them all day long while you're at work to cook them in the evening for dinner.) In warm weather, refrigerate the beans in their soaking liquid. Drain the beans and rinse under cold running water. The beans are now ready for further cooking.

➤ To quick-soak the beans in a pressure cooker (our preference), place the rinsed and sorted beans and cold water in a 5- to 7-quart pressure cooker. For 1 cup dried beans, use 3 cups water; for 1½ cups beans, use 4 cups water; and for 2 cups beans, 6 cups water. Bring to high pressure over high heat. Cook for 2 minutes. Remove from the heat and quick-release the steam. Open the lid, tilting it away from you to block any escaping steam. Drain and rinse the beans under cold running water. The beans are now ready to be cooked.

➤ Never cook or quick-soak more than 1 pound (about 2½ cups) of dried beans at a time in a pressure cooker.

➤ Do not add salt to the soaking water or initial cooking liquid for dried beans. Salt toughens the skins and lengthens the cooking time, sometimes to the point where the beans never cook. Acidic ingredients, such as tomatoes or wine, also toughen bean skins (except for thin-skinned lentils). Salting the beans during their final cooking (after they have softened sufficiently) improves their flavor. If the beans are tender, add salt to their cooking water, and let the beans cool in the salted liquid.

➤ Before giving the beans their final cooking, always drizzle 1 tablespoon vegetable or olive oil to the surface of the cooking liquid to help reduce foaming.

➤ If the cooking liquid sputters through the vent during the quick-release, let the cooker stand for a few minutes, then try again.

➤ If possible, cool the beans in their cooking liquid. This improves their flavor and texture.

➤ Save the cooking liquid from drained beans to use in soups.

➤ Cooked beans taste best if made a day ahead. Stored tightly covered in their cooking liquid, they can be refrigerated for up to 3 days.

➤ When you have a collection of leftover dried beans, combine them to make a favorite bean soup, such as Peasant Cabbage and Bean Soup with Kielbasa on page 31. (Don't use black beans, which will color the whole batch.) Cook the beans until all of them are tender, and don't worry if a few break up.

estimated pressure-cooking times for beans

These estimated times are for quick-soaked beans, pressure-cooked at high pressure, then quick-released. The beans are then simmered, uncovered, in their cooking liquid until tender.

Black (Turtle)	.7 minutes
Black-Eyed Peas*	.5 minutes
Cannellini	.5 minutes
Cranberry	.3 minutes
Garbanzos (Chickpeas)	.18 minutes
Great Northern	.3 minutes
Kidney, Red	.7 minutes
Lentils*	.4 minutes
Lima, Baby	.2 minutes
Navy	.7 minutes
Pink	.7 minutes
Pinto	.7 minutes
Red Beans	.6 minutes

* Do not soak.

basic beans

The chart on page 93 gives estimated cooking times, but be flexible. For 1 cup dried beans, use 3 cups water or stock; for 1½ cups dried beans, use 4 cups; and for 2 cups dried beans, use 6 cups. Beans cook to about twice their dried volume. If desired, season the beans with one small onion (peeled and cut in half for easy removal), a few peeled garlic cloves (no need to remove them after cooking), a bay leaf, and/or ¼ teaspoon dried thyme.

1 cup dried beans, soaked, drained, and rinsed (see page 92)
3 cups water, Homemade Chicken Stock (page 23), or canned low-sodium broth
1 tablespoon vegetable or olive oil
Salt, to taste

1. Place the beans and water or stock in a 5- to 7-quart pressure cooker. Drizzle the oil over the water or stock. Bring to high pressure over high heat. Adjust the heat to maintain the pressure. Cook for the time indicated in the chart on page 93. Remove from the heat and quick-release the pressure.

2. Open the lid, tilting it away from you to block any escaping steam. Check the beans for doneness. If necessary, return the uncovered pot to medium-low heat, season with salt, and bring to a simmer. Cook, testing the beans occasionally, until tender.

3. If possible, cool the beans in their cooking liquid. Drain the beans, saving the cooking liquid to use in soups, if desired.

Makes about 2 cups cooked beans
Cooking time at high pressure depends on bean variety

black beans with chorizo

A little bit of chorizo, a hard, spicy smoked sausage, goes a long way to season a whole pot of beans. You'll find it at Latino markets. (Do not substitute loose-pack chorizo, which resembles ground pork sausage. If necessary, use pepperoni.) Serve the beans with a stack of warm corn or flour tortillas, or spoon over rice.

2 tablespoons olive oil
6 ounces hard chorizo sausage, cut into ½-inch dice
1 large onion, chopped
1 medium red bell pepper, seeded and chopped
1 jalapeño pepper, seeded and finely chopped
2 garlic cloves, finely chopped
2 teaspoons chili powder
½ teaspoon dried oregano
3 cups Homemade Chicken Stock (page 23) or canned low-sodium broth
1 pound dried black beans, soaked and drained (see page 92)
½ teaspoon salt
Salsa (page 79), for serving
Sour cream, for serving
Chopped fresh cilantro, for serving

1. In a 5- to 7-quart pressure cooker, heat 1 tablespoon of the oil over medium heat. Add the chorizo and cook, stirring often, until lightly browned, about 3 minutes. Add the onion, red pepper, jalapeño, and garlic. Cook, stirring often, until the vegetables begin to soften, about 2 minutes. Add the chili powder and oregano and stir until fragrant, about 30 seconds. Stir in the stock and beans. Drizzle the remaining 1 tablespoon oil over the cooking liquid.

2. Lock the lid in place. Bring to high pressure over high heat. Adjust the heat to maintain the pressure. Cook for 7 minutes. Remove from the heat and quick-release the pressure. Open the lid, tilting it away from you to block any escaping steam.

3. Return the cooker to medium heat, stir in the salt, and bring to a simmer. Cook until the beans are tender, mashing some of the beans into the broth to thicken as desired, about 5 minutes.

4. Serve immediately in bowls, with the salsa, sour cream, and cilantro passed on the side for topping.

Makes 8 servings
7 minutes at high pressure

pinto bean salad with chile vinaigrette

This salad is always a hit at summer get-togethers. Bean salads soak up their dressing and usually need to be reseasoned with additional dressing before serving.

VINAIGRETTE

- ¼ cup fresh lime juice
- 2 jalapeño peppers, seeded and minced
- 1 garlic clove, peeled
- 2 teaspoons sugar
- ½ teaspoon salt
- ¼ teaspoon freshly ground black pepper
- 1 cup olive oil

- 1 pound dried pinto beans, cooked, drained, and rinsed (see Basic Beans, page 94)
- 2 medium red bell peppers, roasted and chopped (see Note)
- 4 medium celery ribs, chopped
- 2 cups fresh or thawed corn kernels
- 4 scallions, finely chopped
- Salt and freshly ground black pepper, to taste
- 4 ounces firm goat cheese, such as Bucheron, crumbled (optional)

1. To make the vinaigrette: In a blender, combine the lime juice, jalapeños, garlic, sugar, salt, and pepper. With the machine running, add the oil in a stream until the vinaigrette thickens.

2. In a large bowl, mix the pinto beans, roasted red peppers, celery, corn, and scallions. Toss with ¾ cup of the vinaigrette. Cover and refrigerate until chilled, at least 2 hours.

3. Toss with the remaining ¼ cup vinaigrette. Season with salt and pepper. Top with the cheese, if desired. Serve chilled.

Pinto and Green Bean Salad: Bring a medium saucepan of lightly salted water to a boil over high heat. Add 8 ounces green beans, cut into 1-inch lengths. Cook until crisp-tender, about 3 minutes. Drain and rinse under cold running water. Stir into the salad just before serving.

Note: To roast a red bell pepper, position a broiler rack about 6 inches from the source of heat and preheat the broiler. Cut off the top of the pepper, just below and including the stem, then cut off ½ inch from the bottom. Push out and discard the stem. Slit the pepper down the side, open it up, and cut out the ribs and seeds. Spread out the pepper, skin side up, and press on it to flatten. Broil, skin side up, until the skin is blackened and blistered, 5 to 10 minutes. Be careful not to burn a hole through the pepper—only the skin should blacken. (The flattened pepper can also be grilled over a hot charcoal fire or a gas grill heated to the high setting.) Using kitchen tongs, transfer to a plate and cover with aluminum foil. Let stand until cool enough to handle. Using a small knife, peel and scrape off the skin. Try not to rinse the pepper under cold running water unless absolutely necessary.

Makes 8 to 12 servings
4 minutes at high pressure

cilantro hummus

This is a tasty all-purpose bean spread for serving with crisp pita or baguette toasts as an hors d'oeuvre or to slather onto sandwiches. Substitute other beans for the garbanzo beans if you wish, or other herbs (white beans and sage are an especially good combination).

1 cup dried garbanzo beans (chickpeas), soaked and drained (see page 92)
2 garlic cloves, crushed under a knife and peeled
6 tablespoons extra-virgin olive oil
3 tablespoons fresh lemon juice
½ teaspoon crushed hot red pepper flakes
⅓ cup chopped fresh cilantro leaves
½ teaspoon salt
Chopped cilantro, for garnish (optional)

1. In a 5- to 7-quart pressure cooker, cook the garbanzo beans according to the directions on page 94. Let the beans cool in the cooking liquid. Drain the beans, reserving the cooking liquid.

2. In a food processor fitted with the metal blade, with the machine running, drop the garlic through the feed tube to chop. Add the beans, oil, lemon juice, and hot pepper. With the machine running, gradually pour in enough of the reserved cooking liquid to make a smooth purée, scraping down the sides of the bowl as needed. Add the cilantro leaves and pulse until blended. Season with the salt. Transfer to a serving bowl and sprinkle with the chopped cilantro, if desired. Serve at room temperature.

Makes about 2½ cups
18 minutes at high pressure

garbanzo bean and escarole stew

Another vegetarian main course for bean lovers. It can be made with vegetable stock, but there's really so much flavor from the beans and vegetables that water works just as well. Serve with crusty whole-wheat bread and a crisp green salad, and you're all set.

3 tablespoons extra-virgin olive oil
1 medium red onion, thinly sliced into half-moons
1 medium onion, thinly sliced into half-moons
4 garlic cloves, finely chopped
1 pound garbanzo beans (chickpeas), soaked and drained (see page 92)
6 cups water or canned low-sodium chicken broth
½ teaspoon crushed hot red pepper flakes
One 14½-ounce can tomatoes in juice, drained and chopped
1 teaspoon salt
1 large (1½ pounds) head escarole, well rinsed, torn into large pieces
Freshly grated Parmesan cheese, for serving

1. In a 5- to 7-quart pressure cooker, heat 2 tablespoons of the oil over medium-high heat. Add the onion and cook, stirring often, until golden, about 5 minutes. Add the garlic and stir until fragrant, about 1 minute.

2. Add the beans, water, and hot pepper. Drizzle with the remaining 1 tablespoon oil. Lock the lid in place. Bring to high pressure over high heat. Adjust the heat to maintain the pressure. Cook for 20 minutes. Remove from the heat and quick-release the pressure. Open the lid, tilting it away from you to block any steam.

3. Stir in the tomatoes and salt and bring to a boil, uncovered, over medium-high heat. Gradually stir in the escarole, letting the first batch wilt before adding more. Do not fill the cooker more than two-thirds full. Lock the lid in place and return to high pressure over high heat. Cook for 3 minutes. Remove from the heat, quick-release the pressure, and open the lid.

4. Return to a boil over medium heat, crushing some of the beans against the side of the cooker with a large spoon to thicken the liquid. Serve hot in bowls, with the cheese passed on the side.

■■■■■■■

Makes 8 servings
20 minutes at high pressure for the beans,
then 3 minutes at high pressure for the escarole

cranberry bean, bulgur, and vegetable chili

Here's a rib-sticking chili that is so satisfying you'll never miss the meat. The recipe shows how the beans are almost completely cooked before adding the salt and tomatoes; if added sooner, these ingredients would prevent the beans from softening. Not only does the bulgur thicken the cooking liquid, it combines with the beans to give this vegetarian meal complete protein.

3 tablespoons olive oil
1 large onion, chopped
2 medium carrots, cut into ½-inch-thick rounds
2 medium celery ribs, cut into ½-inch-thick pieces
1 medium red bell pepper, seeded and cut into ½-inch pieces
2 jalapeños, seeded and finely chopped
4 garlic cloves, finely chopped
1 tablespoon chili powder
1½ cups dried cranberry or pinto beans, soaked and drained (see page 92)
3 cups water
One 14½-ounce can tomatoes in juice, drained and chopped
1 cup fresh or thawed frozen corn
1 tablespoon tomato paste
½ teaspoon salt
¾ cup bulgur

1. In a 5- to 7-quart pressure cooker, heat 2 tablespoons of the oil over medium-high heat. Add the onion, carrots, celery, red pepper, jalapeños, and garlic. Cook uncovered, stirring often, until the vegetables are almost tender, about 5 minutes. Add the chili powder and stir until fragrant, about 15 seconds. Transfer the vegetables to a bowl and set aside.

2. Add the beans and water to the pressure cooker. Drizzle with the remaining 1 tablespoon oil. Lock the lid in place. Bring to high pressure over high heat. Adjust the heat to maintain the pressure. Cook for 5 minutes. Remove from the heat and quick-release the pressure. Open the lid, tilting it away from you to block the steam.

3. Stir in the reserved vegetables, tomatoes, corn, tomato paste, and salt. Lock the lid in place, bring back to high pressure over high heat, and adjust the heat to maintain the pressure. Cook for 5 minutes. Remove from the heat, quick-release the pressure, and open the lid.

4. Stir in the bulgur. Cook, uncovered, over medium-low heat until the bulgur is tender and the chili thickens, 3 to 5 minutes. Serve hot.

Makes 8 servings
5 minutes at high pressure for the beans,
then 5 minutes at high pressure for the vegetables

white bean and herb purée

These creamy beans are based on the ones Rick learned to make while working with New York chef Alfred Portale on *The Gotham Bar and Grill Cookbook*. The next time you serve roast pork or leg of lamb, consider them the side dish—we know people who prefer them to mashed potatoes! They can be seasoned with appropriate fresh herbs—try rosemary for lamb, sage for pork, or thyme for either.

1 pound dried cannellini (white kidney) beans, soaked and drained (see page 92)
4 cups Homemade Chicken Stock (page 23) or canned low-sodium broth
1 medium onion, peeled and cut in half lengthwise
3 garlic cloves, crushed under a heavy knife and peeled
⅛ teaspoon dried thyme
1 bay leaf
5 tablespoons extra-virgin olive oil
Salt, to taste
¼ teaspoon freshly ground black pepper

1. In a 5- to 7-quart pressure cooker, combine the beans, stock, onion, garlic, thyme, and bay leaf. Drizzle with 1 tablespoon olive oil. Lock the lid in place. Bring to high pressure over high heat. Adjust the heat to maintain the pressure. Cook for 10 minutes. Remove from the heat and quick-release the pressure. Open the lid, tilting it away from you to block any escaping steam. Discard the onion pieces (they will be on top) and the bay leaf. The beans should be very tender. Drain well in a colander, reserving the cooking liquid for another use, if desired. Return the beans to the cooker and cook uncovered over medium heat, stirring often, to evaporate any excess moisture, about 2 minutes.

2. Transfer to a food processor fitted with the metal blade. Process, gradually adding the remaining 4 tablespoons of oil until the purée is very smooth. Season with salt and the pepper. Serve hot. (The purée can be prepared up to 1 day ahead, cooled, covered, and refrigerated. Reheat over low heat, adding chicken broth to thin to the desired consistency.)

Makes 6 to 8 servings
10 minutes at high pressure

maple and bourbon beans

Baked beans are a summertime favorite, but who likes to turn on the stove when it's hot outside? These pressure-cooked beans will keep you cool and your guests happy. They're best made with supermarket maple-flavored pancake syrup, not pure maple syrup, which has a delicate flavor that will be lost in this hearty dish.

4 bacon strips, coarsely chopped
1 large onion, chopped
2 garlic cloves, finely chopped
6 cups water
1 pound Great Northern beans, soaked and drained (see page 92)
1 tablespoon vegetable oil
½ cup catsup
½ cup maple-flavored pancake syrup
3 tablespoons spicy brown mustard
3 tablespoons light brown sugar
3 tablespoons bourbon whiskey (optional)
Salt, to taste

1. In a 5- to 7-quart pressure cooker, cook the bacon over medium heat, stirring occasionally, until crisp and browned, about 6 minutes. Using a slotted spoon, transfer the bacon to paper towels to drain.

2. Add the onion to the fat in the cooker and cook until the onion is golden, about 5 minutes. Stir in the garlic and cook until fragrant, about 30 seconds. Add the water and beans, and drizzle with the oil.

3. Lock the lid in place. Bring to high pressure over high heat. Adjust the heat to maintain the pressure. Cook for 3 minutes. Remove from the heat and quick-release the pressure. Check the beans for doneness. If necessary, simmer uncovered over medium-low heat until tender. Drain the beans, reserving the cooking liquid for another use, if desired.

4. Return the beans to the cooker. Stir in the reserved bacon, catsup, syrup, mustard, and brown sugar. Cook, uncovered, over medium heat, stirring often, until the mixture thickens slightly, about 5 minutes. Stir in the bourbon if desired. Season with salt. Serve hot.

———

Makes 8 servings
3 minutes at high pressure

new orleans red beans and rice

Very Good!

To this day, red beans and rice is the Monday daily special in many New Orleans restaurants (and homes, too). This tradition started many years ago when Monday was laundry day, and the cook could put on a pot of beans to simmer for hours while she washed the clothes. If we had our way, every cook in New Orleans would have a pressure cooker to make this great meal anytime without setting aside half a day to do it!

    2 tablespoons olive oil
    1 pound andouille or other smoked sausage,
      cut into ½-inch-thick rounds
    1 large onion, chopped
    2 medium celery ribs with leaves, chopped
    1 medium red bell pepper, seeded and chopped
    2 garlic cloves, minced
    1 tablespoon Cajun Seasoning (page 84)
    1 pound dried small red beans, soaked and drained
      (see page 92)
    3 cups Homemade Beef Stock (page 24) or
      canned low-sodium broth
    Salt, to taste
    6 cups hot cooked rice (2 cups raw rice)

1. In a 5- to 7-quart pressure cooker, heat 1 tablespoon of the oil over medium-high heat. Add the sausage and cook, turning occasionally, until lightly browned, about 5 minutes. Add the onion, celery, red pepper, and garlic. Cook, stirring often, until the vegetables begin to soften, about 3 minutes. Stir in the Cajun Seasoning. Add the beans and stock. If necessary, add enough water to the cooker to cover the beans. Drizzle the remaining 1 tablespoon oil on top.

2. Lock the lid in place. Bring to high pressure over high heat. Adjust the heat to maintain the pressure. Cook for 7 minutes. Remove from the heat and quick-release the pressure. Open the lid, tilting it away from you to block any escaping steam.

3. Return the cooker to medium heat and bring to a simmer. Cook until the beans are tender, mashing some beans into the broth to thicken as desired, about 5 minutes. Season with salt.

4. To serve, ladle the beans into soup bowls and top with a spoonful of rice.

Makes 8 servings
7 minutes at high pressure

risotto and grains

When pressure cooking began its resurgence a few years ago, pressure-cooked risotto was the big surprise. Everyone expected the pressure cooker to turn out great stew, but risotto…? The delicate darling of Italian restaurants? The famous rice dish that requires constant stirring and attention, banishing the home cook to the kitchen to slave away while ignoring the guests in the living room?

Yes, you can make terrific risotto in 6 minutes in the pressure cooker. The steam and pressure combine to make a no-stir risotto that isn't just passable, it's *great!* With these recipes and a pressure cooker, risotto is likely to become a standard meal at your house.

The pressure cooker does a fine job with other grains, too. We've concentrated on the ones that we think you'll cook most often. We save the pressure cooker to prepare long-cooking grains like brown rice and wild rice. For plain white rice, most manufacturers recommend low pressure, and many models come with only a high setting. Besides, long-grain rice takes only 15 minutes to cook. We would rather have our pressure cooker free for making the main course and prepare the rice in a traditional saucepan. However, we do make a one-pot meal, Spanish Rice with Sausage (page 112), with long-grain rice in the pressure cooker.

tips for risotto

➤ To make risotto, you must use a medium-grain rice. This rice contains sufficient starch to give risotto its creamy texture. The most popular rice for risotto is Arborio, from Italy (there is also a California-grown Arborio); however, it is popular mainly because it is relatively easy to grow and has flooded the market. If you can find them, Carnaroli and Vialone Nano varieties have superior texture and flavor, and while somewhat expensive, they are worth the extra money.

➤ The exact cooking time varies with different brands of rice. When you find a brand you like, stick with it. If the risotto needs more cooking (it should be al dente, but not hard), stir in about ½ cup of broth and simmer uncovered over medium-low heat, stirring almost constantly, until the rice is the desired texture and the cooking liquid has a loose, creamy consistency.

➤ The risotto recipes can be halved to make fewer servings. You do not have to use a different-sized pot.

➤ A 2½-quart skillet-shaped cooker is the ideal utensil for pressure-cooked risotto. If you love risotto, you'll want to have one of these cookers. However, any 5- to 7-quart cooker will do the job.

➤ If you wish, stir an additional 2 tablespoons of butter into the risotto just before serving. It adds an exquisite richness, though it is an indulgence.

risotto with green apples

This is an unusual, but delicious, side dish for Osso Bucco Presto (page 71) or as an opening course to an autumn dinner. If you don't have two pressure cookers, make the osso bucco and keep warm in a 200°F oven while making the risotto.

- 4 tablespoons unsalted butter
- 1 small onion, chopped
- 1 garlic clove, finely chopped
- 2 tablespoons fresh lemon juice
- ¾ cup rice for risotto (Arborio, Carnaroli, or Vialone Nano)
- 1½ cups Homemade Chicken Stock (page 23) or canned low-sodium broth, plus more as needed
- ¼ teaspoon salt, plus more to taste
- ⅛ teaspoon freshly ground black pepper, plus more to taste
- 1 large tart apple, such as Granny Smith, cut into ¼-inch dice
- ⅓ cup freshly grated Parmesan cheese

1. In a 5- to 7-quart pressure cooker, heat 2 tablespoons of the butter over medium heat. Add the onion and cook until it begins to soften, about 2 minutes. Add the garlic and cook for 30 more seconds. Add the lemon juice and cook until evaporated, about 1 minute. Add the rice and stir constantly until it is well coated with butter, but not browned, about 1 minute. Stir in the stock, ¼ teaspoon salt, and ⅛ teaspoon pepper.

2. Lock the lid in place. Bring to high pressure over high heat. Adjust the heat to maintain pressure. Cook for 6 minutes. Remove from the heat and quick-release the pressure. Open the lid, tilting it away from you to block any escaping steam. Taste the risotto; it should be barely tender (al dente). If necessary, return to medium-low heat, add ½ cup broth or water, and stir until the rice is tender.

3. Stir in the apples and cheese. Stir in the remaining 2 tablespoons butter. Season with additional salt and pepper. Serve immediately.

Makes 6 side-dish servings
6 minutes at high pressure

shrimp and saffron risotto

The shrimp for this elegant and easy risotto are cut lengthwise into two thin halves. This allows them to be better distributed throughout the dish. However, take care not to overcook them, because after their initial sauté, they will be reheated in the hot risotto. In some parts of Italy where cheese is scarce but fish is abundant, cooks warn against serving cheese with fish or shellfish. This dictum evolved for agricultural and geographical reasons rather than culinary good sense (as cheese and fish can be delicious together), so add the Parmesan, if you wish.

4 tablespoons unsalted butter
1 pound medium shrimp, peeled (save shells for stock, if desired), deveined, and cut in halves lengthwise
¼ teaspoon crumbled saffron threads
½ cup dry white wine
1 medium onion, chopped
2 garlic cloves, minced
1½ cups rice for risotto (Arborio, Carnaroli, or Vialone Nano)
3½ cups Shrimp Stock (recipe follows), or 1½ cups canned low-sodium chicken broth, 1 cup bottled clam juice, and 1 cup water, plus more broth or water as needed
½ teaspoon salt, plus more to taste
¼ teaspoon freshly ground black pepper, plus more to taste
1 large ripe tomato, seeded and cut into ½-inch cubes
2 tablespoons chopped fresh parsley
Freshly grated Parmesan cheese, for serving

1. In a 5- to 7-quart pressure cooker, melt 2 tablespoons of the butter over medium heat. Add the shrimp and cook just until they turn pink, about 2 minutes. Using a slotted spoon, transfer the shrimp to a plate and set aside.

2. Stir the saffron into the wine and set aside. Add the remaining 2 tablespoons butter to the pot and heat over medium heat. Add the onion and garlic and cook just until beginning to soften, about 1 minute. Add the rice and stir constantly until it is well coated with butter but not browned, about 1 minute. Add the saffron-wine and cook until it is almost completely evaporated, about 2 minutes. Stir in the shrimp stock and season with ½ teaspoon salt and ¼ teaspoon pepper.

3. Lock the lid in place. Bring to high pressure over high heat. Adjust the heat to maintain pressure. Cook for 6 minutes. Remove from the heat and quick-release the pressure. Open the lid, tilting it away from you to block any escaping steam. Taste the risotto; it should be barely tender (al dente). If necessary, return to medium-low heat, add ½ cup water, and stir until the rice is tender. Just before serving, stir in the shrimp, tomato, and parsley. Season with additional salt and pepper. Serve immediately, with the cheese passed on the side.

Shrimp Stock: In a 5- to 7-quart pressure cooker, combine the shells from 1 pound shrimp, 3 cups water, 1 cup bottled clam juice or canned low-sodium chicken broth, 1 small onion and 1 small celery rib with leaves (both chopped), 4 parsley sprigs, ¼ teaspoon dried thyme, and ¼ teaspoon whole black peppercorns. Lock the lid in place. Bring to high pressure over high heat. Adjust the heat to maintain the pressure. Cook for 5 minutes. Quick-release the pressure. Strain the stock into a medium bowl. Yield: About 3½ cups.

Makes 4 main-course or 6 to 8 first-course servings
6 minutes at high pressure

risotto with porcini and parmesan

Arlene makes this risotto all the time for a quick supper. She believes that every kitchen should be stocked with basic staples that allow a cook to make impromptu meals. She is never without the Italian rice, dried mushrooms, canned broth, or Parmesan cheese to make this satisfying dish. (And if you have some gorgonzola or other blue cheese on hand, toss that in, too.)

1 ounce (1 cup) dried porcini mushrooms
4 tablespoons unsalted butter
1 medium onion, chopped
2 garlic cloves, minced
1½ cups rice for risotto (Arborio, Carnaroli, or Vialone Nano)
½ cup dry white wine
2 cups boiling water
1½ cups Homemade Chicken Stock (page 23) or canned low-sodium broth, plus more as needed
½ cup freshly grated Parmesan cheese
½ cup crumbled Gorgonzola cheese (optional)
Salt and freshly ground black pepper, to taste

1. Rinse the dried mushrooms under cold running water to remove any grit. Chop coarsely and set aside.

2. In a 5- to 7-quart pressure cooker, melt 2 tablespoons of the butter over medium heat. Add the onion and cook until softened, about 3 minutes. Stir in the reserved mushrooms and the garlic and cook for 30 seconds. Add the rice and stir constantly until the rice is well-coated with butter but not browned, about 1 minute. Add the wine and cook until it is almost completely evaporated, about 2 minutes. Add the water and broth.

3. Lock the lid in place. Bring to high pressure over high heat. Adjust the heat to maintain pressure. Cook for 6 minutes. Remove from the heat and quick-release the pressure. Open the lid, tilting it away from you to block any escaping steam. Taste the risotto; it should be barely tender (al dente). If necessary, return to medium-low heat, add ½ cup broth or water, and stir until the rice is tender and the liquid is creamy. Stir in the Parmesan cheese, and Gorgonzola if desired. Stir in the remaining 2 tablespoons butter. Season with salt and pepper. Serve immediately.

Risotto with Two Mushrooms: In a large skillet, heat 2 tablespoons unsalted butter over medium heat. Add one large portobello mushroom, chopped into ½-inch cubes. Cook until the mushroom is tender, about 6 minutes. Season with salt and pepper. Stir the cooked portobello mushroom into the risotto just before serving.

Makes 4 main-course or 6 to 8 first-course servings
6 minutes at high pressure

spanish rice with sausage

When Arlene's kids were growing up, this was one of their favorite meals, and she always made it in the pressure cooker. It is still popular with the kids in our families. If you wish, stir ½ cup thawed petite peas and a couple of tablespoons chopped fresh basil into the rice just before serving.

2 tablespoons olive oil
1 medium onion, chopped
2 medium celery ribs, chopped
1 garlic clove, finely chopped
1 pound sweet Italian pork or turkey sausage,
   casings removed
1½ cups long-grain rice
¼ teaspoon dried oregano
¼ teaspoon salt
¼ teaspoon freshly ground black pepper
2½ cups Homemade Chicken Stock (page 23)
   or canned low-sodium broth
One 14½-ounce can tomatoes in juice, drained
   and chopped, juices reserved

1. In a 5- to 7-quart pressure cooker, heat the oil over medium-high heat. Add the onion, celery, and garlic. Cook, stirring often, until the vegetables begin to soften, about 2 minutes. Add the sausage and cook, breaking it up with the side of a spoon, until it loses its raw look, about 7 minutes. Pour off any excess fat from the cooker.

2. Add the rice, oregano, salt, and pepper and stir well. Add the stock and the tomatoes and their juice.

3. Lock the lid in place. Bring to high pressure over high heat. Adjust the heat to maintain the pressure. Cook for 6 minutes. Remove from the heat and quick-release the pressure. Open the lid, tilting it away from you to block any escaping steam. Stir well. Serve immediately.

Makes 6 main-course servings
6 minutes at high pressure

RISOTTO AND GRAINS

brown rice pilaf with peas

Brown rice is another grain that takes just a little too much time to cook often by traditional cooking methods. The pressure cooker reduces the time, but brown rice tends to foam, so add oil to the cooking liquid.

1 tablespoon unsalted butter
1 medium onion, chopped
2 cups long-grain brown rice
3½ cups Homemade Chicken Stock (page 23)
  or canned low-sodium broth
1 bay leaf
½ teaspoon salt
⅛ teaspoon freshly ground black pepper
1 tablespoon vegetable oil
1 cup frozen petite peas, rinsed under hot water
  to thaw
½ cup freshly grated Parmesan cheese

1. In a 5- to 7-quart pressure cooker, melt the butter over medium heat. Add the onion and cook, stirring often, until it begins to soften, about 2 minutes. Add the brown rice and cook, stirring often, until well coated with the butter, about 1 minute. Add the stock, bay leaf, salt, and pepper. Drizzle with the oil.

2. Lock the lid in place. Bring to high pressure over high heat. Adjust the heat to maintain the pressure. Cook for 20 minutes. Remove from the heat and quick-release the pressure.

3. Open the lid, tilting it away from you to block any escaping steam. Remove the bay leaf. Stir in the peas and cheese. Serve hot.

Makes 6 side-dish servings
20 minutes at high pressure

risotto with butternut squash and sausage

This satisfying risotto may be too rich for a first course unless the entrée is something quite light (we like to serve it as an opener to grilled fish).

1 pound (½ medium) butternut squash, peeled, seeded, and cut into 1-inch cubes

4 tablespoons unsalted butter

1 pound sweet Italian pork sausage, casings removed

1 medium onion, chopped

1½ cups rice for risotto (Arborio, Carnaroli, or Vialone Nano)

½ cup dry white wine

3½ cups Homemade Chicken Stock (page 23) or canned low-sodium broth, plus more as needed

¼ teaspoon salt, plus more to taste

¼ teaspoon freshly ground black pepper, plus more to taste

½ cup freshly grated Parmesan cheese

A few gratings of fresh nutmeg

Chopped fresh sage, for garnish

1. Place the trivet and steaming basket in a 5- to 7-quart pressure cooker. Add 2 cups water to the cooker. Place the squash in the basket. Lock the lid in place. Bring to high pressure over high heat. Cook for 1½ minutes. Remove from the heat and quick-release the pressure. Open the lid, tilting it away from you to block any escaping steam. Remove the squash from the cooker and set aside.

2. Rinse and dry the cooker. Add 2 tablespoons of the butter to the cooker and melt over medium heat. Add the sausage and onion and cook, stirring often and breaking up the sausage with a spoon, until the sausage loses its raw look, about 6 minutes. Do not brown the sausage. Pour off all but 2 tablespoons of the fat. Add the rice and cook, stirring often, until well-coated, about 2 minutes. Add the wine and bring to a boil. Stir in the stock, ¼ teaspoon salt, and ¼ teaspoon pepper.

3. Lock the lid in place. Bring to high pressure over high heat. Adjust the heat to maintain pressure. Cook for 6 minutes. Remove from the heat and quick-release the pressure. Open the lid, tilting it away from you to block any escaping steam. Taste the risotto; it should be barely tender (al dente). If necessary, return to medium-low heat, add ½ cup stock or water, and stir until the rice is tender and the liquid is creamy. Stir in the reserved squash, Parmesan cheese, and the remaining 2 tablespoons butter. Season with the nutmeg and additional salt and pepper. Serve immediately, garnishing each serving with the sage.

Makes 4 main-course or 6 to 8 first-course servings
1½ minutes at high pressure for the squash, then
6 minutes at high pressure for the risotto

holiday **wild rice** with dried cranberries

Aside dish that goes well with holiday poultry main dishes like turkey, goose, or duck, this wild rice is studded with dried cranberries. Wild rice isn't a rice at all, but a type of grass. Wild rice from the Great Lakes region is usually hand-harvested by traditional methods. It tends to be firmer than the machine-harvested varieties from other states. (The hand-harvested wild rice is more expensive, too.) Even when cooked in a normal pot, the cooking time for wild rice is hard to predict, so be flexible. If you wish, stir ¾ cup chopped toasted pecans into the rice just before serving.

1 tablespoon unsalted butter
⅓ cup chopped shallots
1½ cups (11 ounces) wild rice, rinsed under cold
   water
4½ cups Homemade Chicken Stock (page 23)
   or canned low-sodium broth
¼ teaspoon dried thyme
½ teaspoon salt
¼ teaspoon freshly ground black pepper
½ cup dried cranberries or dried cherries

1. In a 5- to 7-quart pressure cooker, melt the butter over medium heat. Add the shallots and cook until they begin to soften, about 1 minute. Add the wild rice, stock, thyme, salt, and pepper.

2. Lock the lid in place. Bring to high pressure over high heat. Adjust the heat to maintain the pressure. Cook for 30 minutes. Remove from the heat and quick-release the pressure. Open the lid, tilting it away from you to block any escaping steam. The wild rice should be tender and puffed. If necessary, attach the lid and cook over high pressure for an additional 5 minutes. Off heat, add the dried cranberries and let stand for 5 minutes. Drain well. Transfer to a serving dish and serve hot.

Makes 6 to 8 side-dish servings
30 minutes at high pressure

polenta with **gorgonzola**

If you have a pressure cooker with a nonstick lining, you'll never have to stir a pot of polenta again. (Unfortunately, polenta sticks to regular pots.) For the best texture, use coarse-grain cornmeal or imported Italian polenta. (Don't confuse it with instant polenta.) For a main course, substitute ½ cup freshly grated Parmesan cheese for the gorgonzola, and spoon Wild Mushroom Sauce (page 124) over the polenta.

> 2 cups Homemade Chicken Stock (page 23)
>   or canned low-sodium broth
> ¼ teaspoon salt, plus more to taste
> 1 cup coarse-grain cornmeal
> 1 cup water
> 1 tablespoon olive oil
> 3 ounces Gorgonzola or other blue-veined cheese,
>   crumbled
> ¼ teaspoon freshly ground black pepper

1. In a nonstick 5- to 7-quart pressure cooker, bring the stock and ¼ teaspoon salt to a boil over high heat. In a medium bowl, whisk the cornmeal and water together, then whisk into the boiling broth. Drizzle the top with the olive oil.

2. Lock the lid in place. Using a heat diffuser, bring to high pressure over high heat. Cook for 2 minutes. Remove from the heat and quick-release the pressure. Open the lid, tilting it away from you to block any escaping steam. Add the gorgonzola and pepper, and stir to melt the cheese. Season with additional salt. Serve immediately.

Makes 4 to 6 side-dish servings
2 minutes at high pressure

wheat berries with carrots and currants

Wheat berries make a splendid side dish, but their long cooking time discourages most cooks from serving them often. The pressure cooker will change that for you. Most natural food stores carry soft and hard wheat berries—soft berries will cook more quickly. For a real treat, substitute farro (see Note below). To further reduce the cooking time, soak the wheat berries in cold water for 4 to 8 hours, and drain. Carrots and currants enhance the berries' natural sweetness. This dish is wonderful prepared as a stovetop "stuffing" for roast chicken. If you like, add chopped fresh thyme or dill to the finished dish.

1 tablespoon olive oil
1 medium onion, chopped
1 medium carrot, cut into ½-inch dice
1 cup (7 ounces) soft wheat berries
½ teaspoon salt, plus more to taste
¼ teaspoon freshly ground black pepper, plus
   more to taste
2 cups Homemade Chicken Stock (page 23) or
   canned low-sodium broth
1 cup water
⅓ cup dried currants

1. In a 5- to 7-quart pressure cooker, heat the oil over medium heat. Add the onion and carrot and cook until the vegetables begin to soften, about 2 minutes. Add the wheat berries, ½ teaspoon salt, and ¼ teaspoon pepper. Cook, stirring often, for 1 minute. Add the stock and water.

2. Lock the lid in place. Bring to high pressure over high heat. Adjust the heat to maintain the pressure. Cook for 35 minutes. Remove from the heat and quick-release the pressure. Open the lid, tilting it away from you to block any escaping steam. The berries should be chewy-tender. If not, simmer over low heat, uncovered, to reach the desired tenderness. Off heat, add the currants and let stand for 5 minutes. Drain well.

3. Return the drained wheat berries to the cooker. Cook over medium heat, uncovered, stirring almost constantly, to evaporate excess moisture, about 1 minute. Season with additional salt and pepper. Serve hot.

Note: Farro, an ancient wheat variety related to spelt, has been recently discovered by chefs and home cooks. It's expensive, but with its full, earthy flavor, you'll probably become a fan, too. Look for it at specialty food stores and Italian grocers. Cook as directed above, but delete the currants (to better appreciate the farro's taste). Or, cook and stir in freshly grated Parmesan cheese and peas, as suggested for the Brown Rice Pilaf with Peas on page 113.

Makes 4 to 6 side-dish servings
35 minutes at high pressure

quick pasta sauces

You've just rushed in from work, and you're famished. You want something easy to cook, a no-brainer. If you're anything like us, a lot of the time you make a pot of pasta. And it's no compromise, because you love it! It's the pasta sauce that takes some time to pull together, at least if you want that "simmering on the back of the stove for hours like the one Grandma used to make" flavor. (Assuming that Grandma was Italian.)

The bad news is that you gain nothing by cooking pasta in a pressure cooker. (Most manufacturers warn against doing so, and while some intrepid cooks have figured out ways to do it without hurting themselves, we say it's not worth the hassle.) The good news is that you can make *bellissimo* sauces in the pressure cooker in the amount of time it takes for the water to come to a boil and cook the pasta.

The sauces in this chapter call for 1 pound of cooked pasta. If yours is a smaller family, use half of the sauce with 8 ounces of pasta, and freeze the rest for another meal. You'll have a treasure trove of frozen sauce to thaw in the microwave for the next time you come home from work hassled and hurried.

three-meat **bolognese** sauce

Bolognese sauce, enhanced with a bit of cream, is one of the most glorious concoctions you can put on pasta. This sauce is all about meat—you may notice that it doesn't have the herbs associated with most pasta sauces. We use a meat-loaf mixture (equal parts of beef, veal, and pork) to give it a delicate, but rich, flavor. Instead of cooking your sauce for hours, pressure-cook it for 15 minutes, and take pride in the speedy but tasty result. It is particularly luscious with fresh fettucine.

1 tablespoon unsalted butter
1 medium onion, chopped
1 medium carrot, chopped
1 medium celery rib with leaves, chopped
1 garlic clove, minced
1½ pounds meat-loaf mixture, or 8 ounces each ground round, ground pork, and ground veal
½ cup dry white wine, such as Pinot Grigio or Sauvignon Blanc
One 14½-ounce can tomatoes in juice, drained and chopped, juices reserved
2 tablespoons tomato paste
1 bay leaf
½ teaspoon salt
¼ teaspoon freshly ground black pepper
½ cup heavy cream

1. In a 5- to 7-quart pressure cooker, melt the butter over medium-high heat. Add the onion, carrot, celery, and garlic. Cook, stirring occasionally, until the vegetables begin to soften, about 2 minutes. Add the meat-loaf mixture and cook, breaking up the meat with a spoon, until the meat loses its pink color, about 5 minutes. Pour off the excess fat from the pot. (If desired, drain the meat and vegetables in a wire sieve, and return the solids to the pot.)

2. Add the wine and boil until reduced by about half, about 2 minutes. Stir in the chopped tomatoes and their juice, tomato paste, bay leaf, salt, and pepper. Lock the lid in place. Bring to high pressure over high heat. Adjust the heat to maintain the pressure. Cook for 15 minutes.

3. Remove from the heat and quick-release the pressure. Open the lid, tilting it away from you to block any escaping steam. Return the uncovered pot to medium-high heat and bring the sauce to a boil. Add the cream and cook until the sauce is slightly thickened, about 5 minutes.

━━━━━━━━━━━

Makes about 4 cups sauce
15 minutes at high pressure

summer tomato and **basil** sauce

Plum tomatoes make the best tomato sauce. (Large beefsteak tomatoes are great sliced in salads, but are too juicy for the saucepot.) The seeds must be removed or the sauce will be too thin, yet the skins are kept on to give the sauce body. You'll need only ¼ cup water to get the sauce to come up to pressure, as the tomatoes give off juice as they cook. (In fact, you may not need any water at all. Try to bring the sauce up to pressure without the water, and add the water only if pressure isn't reached.) Instead of Parmesan cheese, drizzle each serving of pasta with a little extra olive oil.

to a food processor fitted with the metal blade and purée. Add the basil and pulse to combine. Season with the salt.

—————————

Makes about 4 cups sauce
6 minutes at high pressure

1 tablespoon extra-virgin olive oil
2 garlic cloves
4 pounds ripe plum tomatoes, cut in half
   lengthwise and squeezed gently to remove seeds
¼ cup water, optional (see above)
¼ teaspoon crushed hot red pepper flakes
½ cup chopped fresh basil
½ teaspoon salt

1. In a 5- to 7-quart pressure cooker, heat the oil over medium heat. Add the garlic and cook, stirring often, until softened, about 1 minute. Stir in the tomatoes, water, if desired, and hot pepper.

2. Lock the lid in place. Bring to high pressure over high heat. Adjust the heat to maintain the pressure. Cook for 6 minutes. Remove from the heat and quick-release the pressure. Open the lid, tilting it away from you to block any escaping steam.

3. Return the cooker to medium heat. Boil the sauce, uncovered, stirring often until slightly thickened, about 5 minutes. Transfer the tomato mixture

sicilian tomato and **pork** sauce

This is a light-bodied meat-infused sauce that clings well to pasta—try it with ziti or rigatoni. The secret ingredient is pork neck bones, which are available at most supermarkets (at least the ones that cater to smart ethnic cooks who know that pork neck bones pack a lot of flavor for very little money). Serve the pasta with plenty of freshly grated Parmesan or Romano cheese.

3 tablespoons olive oil
2 pounds pork neck bones, sawed into large pieces
1 large onion, chopped
2 garlic cloves, minced
1 teaspoon dried oregano
1 teaspoon dried basil
1/8 teaspoon crushed hot red pepper flakes
1 bay leaf
1/2 cup hearty red wine, such as Zinfandel
One 28-ounce can crushed tomatoes
Salt, to taste

1. In a 5- to 7-quart pressure cooker, heat 2 tablespoons of the oil over medium-high heat. In batches, add the neck bones and cook until browned on both sides, about 4 minutes. Transfer to a plate and set aside.

2. Add the remaining 1 tablespoon oil to the pot and heat. Add the onion and garlic and cook until softened, about 2 minutes. Stir in the oregano, basil, crushed red pepper, and bay leaf. Add the wine and boil until reduced by half, about 2 minutes. Stir in the tomatoes. Return the pork bones to the pot.

3. Lock the lid in place. Bring to high pressure over high heat. Adjust the heat to maintain the pressure. Cook for 40 minutes. Remove from the heat and quick-release the pressure. Open the lid, tilting it away from you to block any escaping steam.

4. Transfer the bones to a cutting board. Using a fork, pull the meat from the bones (don't worry about getting every last morsel—just the substantial pieces are enough) and discard the bones. Shred the meat and return to the sauce. Season the sauce with salt.

Sicilian Tomato and Ricotta Pasta: Toss the sauce with one pound cooked pasta and one 15-ounce container ricotta cheese, at room temperature. (Chilled ricotta will cool the pasta too much.)

Makes about 4 cups sauce
40 minutes at high pressure

wild mushroom sauce

Here's a quick pasta sauce with deep, earthy flavors. It's best on sturdy pasta, like ziti or rigatoni. Dried mushrooms are usually soaked for 20 minutes or so to soften before cooking, but that step is unnecessary with a pressure cooker.

1 cup (1 ounce) dried porcini mushrooms
2 tablespoons olive oil
1 medium onion, chopped
2 garlic cloves, finely chopped
1 pound fresh white mushrooms, sliced
1 cup boiling Homemade Chicken Stock (page 23) or canned low-sodium broth
One 14½-ounce can tomatoes in juice, drained and chopped
2 tablespoons tomato paste
¼ teaspoon dried rosemary
¼ teaspoon dried sage
¼ teaspoon salt
¼ teaspoon freshly ground black pepper
2 tablespoons chopped fresh parsley

1. Rinse the dried mushrooms under cold running water to remove the grit. Chop coarsely and set aside.

2. In a 5- to 7-quart pressure cooker, heat the oil over medium heat. Add the onion and garlic and cook, stirring often, until the vegetables begin to soften, about 2 minutes. Add the fresh mushrooms and cook, stirring often, until softened, about 5 minutes. Stir in the broth, the tomatoes, tomato paste, rosemary, sage, salt, and pepper.

3. Lock the lid in place. Bring to high pressure over high heat. Adjust the heat to maintain the pressure. Cook for 5 minutes. Remove from the heat and quick-release the pressure. Open the lid, tilting it away from you to block any escaping steam. Stir in the parsley.

Makes about 3½ cups sauce
5 minutes at high pressure

spaghetti and meatballs

I t's pretty safe to say that everyone loves spaghetti and meatballs, especially kids. This pressure-cooked version brings this crowd-pleaser on the table in under 30 minutes, from start to finish (depending on how long it takes for the pasta water to come to a boil). There is only one way to mix the meatball mixture: use your hands, well-washed before and after mixing, of course.

SAUCE
- 1 tablespoon olive oil
- 1 medium onion, chopped
- 2 garlic cloves, finely chopped
- One 28-ounce can crushed tomatoes
- ½ teaspoon dried basil
- ½ teaspoon dried oregano
- ¼ teaspoon crushed hot red pepper flakes

MEATBALLS
- ½ cup fresh Italian or French bread crumbs (make in a blender or food processor)
- ¼ cup milk
- 1½ pounds meat loaf mixture, or 8 ounces each ground round, ground pork, and ground veal
- 1 small onion, finely chopped
- 1 garlic clove, finely chopped
- 1 large egg, beaten
- ½ teaspoon dried basil
- ½ teaspoon salt
- ⅛ teaspoon freshly ground black pepper

- 1 pound spaghetti, cooked
- Freshly grated Parmesan cheese, for serving

1. To make the sauce: In a 5- to 7-quart pressure cooker, heat the oil over medium-high heat. Add the onion and garlic. Cook, stirring often, until the onion begins to soften, about 2 minutes. Stir in the tomatoes, basil, oregano, and hot pepper.

2. Bring to high pressure over high heat. Adjust the heat to maintain the pressure. Cook for 15 minutes. Remove from the heat and quick-release the pressure. Open the lid, tilting it away from you to block any escaping steam. Return the uncovered pot to medium-high heat and bring the sauce to a boil.

3. Meanwhile, prepare the meatballs: In a medium bowl, mix the bread crumbs and milk; let stand 5 minutes. Add the meat-loaf mixture, onion, garlic, egg, basil, salt, and pepper. Using your hands, mix thoroughly. Using about 2 tablespoons for each meatball, form into 2-inch balls.

4. One at a time, place the meatballs in the simmering sauce, shaking the pan as needed to get the meatballs to fit (as much as possible) in one layer. Lock the lid in place. Bring to high pressure over high heat. Adjust the heat to maintain the pressure and cook for 5 minutes. Remove from the heat and quick-release the pressure. Open the lid, tilting it away from you to block any escaping steam.

5. Using a slotted spoon, transfer the meatballs to a plate. In a large bowl, toss the spaghetti with the sauce, then top with the meatballs. Serve immediately, with the cheese passed on the side.

Makes 6 servings
15 minutes at high pressure for sauce,
then 5 minutes at high pressure for meatballs

broccoli rabe and sausage sauce

Broccoli rabe, also called rapini, used to be found only in Italian-neighborhood grocers. Now it has gone mainstream, although in some areas you will find it only during the winter months. With its long, thin stems and leafy florets, broccoli rabe looks like regular broccoli in need of a barber. It has a bracing, slightly bitter flavor that is best tempered with sausage and plenty of garlic. The pressure cooker makes short work out of the traditionally lengthy cooking time. This sauce doesn't freeze well, so toss it right after cooking with hot ziti or rigatoni, and offer Parmesan cheese on the side.

2 tablespoons olive oil

1 pound sweet Italian pork sausage, casings removed

2 garlic cloves, chopped

2 pounds broccoli rabe

1 cup Homemade Chicken Stock (page 23) or canned low-sodium broth

¼ teaspoon crushed hot red pepper

Salt, to taste

1. In a 5- to 7-quart pressure cooker, heat the oil over medium heat. Add the sausage and cook, breaking up with the side of a spoon, until the sausage loses its pink look, about 5 minutes. Add the garlic and cook for 1 minute.

2. While the sausage is cooking, rinse the broccoli rabe well. Shake off excess water but do not dry completely. Cut the stems into ½-inch-long pieces, and coarsely chop the florets. Set aside.

3. In 3 or 4 batches, stir in the broccoli rabe, letting the first batch wilt somewhat before adding another. Pour in the stock and add the crushed red pepper. Lock the lid in place. Bring to high pressure over high heat. Adjust the heat to maintain the pressure. Cook for 5 minutes. Remove from the heat and quick-release the steam. Open the lid, tilting it away from you to block any escaping steam. Season with the salt.

Makes 4 to 6 servings
5 minutes at high pressure

vegetables

When gathering vegetable dishes for this book, we decided to stick to the ones that required long cooking and would benefit from pressure cooking. In our experience, cooking times for the more delicate vegetables vary from cooker to cooker, and it is best to follow the instructions in your cooker's manual. Besides, you probably don't need a "recipe" for steamed carrots tossed with butter. (We do provide instructions for some simple potato dishes, because there are specific ways to prepare them to ensure success.) Also, these days, the cooked texture of many favorite vegetables (broccoli, carrots, and others) is a matter of taste. Some like them crisp-tender, and others well done. It is easier to gauge doneness in a traditional pot. The vegetables we've included here are all at their best when cooked until tender, so there's a minimum of guesswork.

tips for vegetables

➤ Use fresh, flavorful vegetables. Any off-flavors will be intensified in the cooker.

➤ When cooking potatoes, cut them into uniform pieces. Whole potatoes, even small new potatoes, tend to crack and cook unevenly in the pressure cooker.

artichokes with minted vegetable broth

If you have been disappointed by bland pressure-cooked artichokes, as we have, this recipe is for you. The problem is solved by pressure-cooking the artichokes over a delicious broth, which adds much-needed flavor. The broth is served with the artichokes as a dipping sauce, and is so tasty you'll want to serve it with crusty bread. It is important to use medium-sized artichokes, as large ones rarely seem to be cooked through to the heart even though the leaves are tender.

Four medium (8 ounces each) artichokes
1 lemon, halved crosswise
1 tablespoon extra-virgin olive oil, plus more for serving
1 medium onion, chopped
1 medium carrot, chopped
1 medium celery rib with leaves, chopped
2 garlic cloves, minced
1 cup Homemade Chicken Stock (page 23) or canned low-sodium broth
¼ teaspoon salt
2 tablespoons chopped fresh mint
Crusty Italian bread, for serving

1. Using a heavy knife, cut off the stems and top inch from each artichoke. If desired, using kitchen shears, snip the prickly tips from the leaves. Rub the cut surfaces with the lemon. Set aside.

2. In a 5- to 7-quart pressure cooker, heat 1 tablespoon of the oil over medium heat. Add the onion, carrot, celery, and garlic. Cook, stirring often, until the vegetables begin to soften, about 2 minutes. Add the stock and salt and bring to a boil. Place the trivet and steamer basket in the cooker. Stack the artichokes in the basket, pyramid-style.

3. Lock the lid in place. Bring to high pressure over high heat. Adjust the heat to maintain the pressure. Cook for 15 minutes. Remove from the heat and quick-release the pressure. Open the lid, tilting it away from you to block any escaping steam.

4. Using kitchen tongs, place each artichoke in a deep soup bowl. Stir the mint into the broth. Ladle the broth around the artichokes. Serve hot, with the bread passed on the side to sop up the juices, and a cruet of oil for drizzling.

Makes 4 servings
15 minutes at high pressure

german **red cabbage** with bacon and apples

O f course, in the old days, almost every kitchen had a pot of rendered bacon fat (gathered from the daily fried breakfast bacon) in the refrigerator. Now, we cook a few strips of bacon for the recipe to lend its smoky, meaty flavor to the cabbage. Serve this classic with grilled pork chops (smoked chops are especially good). The red wine and vinegar are essential to keep the cabbage from losing its color.

1 tablespoon vegetable oil

3 bacon strips, coarsely chopped

1 medium onion, chopped

2 Granny Smith apples, peeled, seeded, and cut lengthwise into quarters

½ cup fruity red wine, such as Merlot

⅓ cup packed light brown sugar

3 tablespoons red wine vinegar

One medium (2½ pounds) red cabbage, cored and cut into ¼-inch-wide strips

½ teaspoon salt, plus more to taste

¼ teaspoon freshly ground black pepper, plus more to taste

1. In a 5- to 7-quart pressure cooker, heat the oil over medium heat. Add the bacon and cook, stirring occasionally, until crisp and brown, about 5 minutes. Using a slotted spoon, transfer the bacon to paper towels to drain. Pour off all but 2 tablespoons of the fat from the cooker.

2. Return the cooker to medium heat. Add the onion and apples. Cook, uncovered, until the onion begins to soften, about 2 minutes. Stir in the wine, brown sugar, and vinegar and bring to a boil. Gradually stir the cabbage into the cooker, letting each addition wilt before adding another. The cooker should not be more than half-filled. Season with ½ teaspoon salt and ¼ teaspoon pepper.

3. Lock the lid in place. Bring to high pressure over high heat. Adjust the heat to maintain the pressure. Cook for 8 minutes. Remove from the heat and quick-release the pressure. Open the lid, tilting it away from you to block any escaping steam. Season with additional salt and pepper.

4. Using a slotted spoon, transfer the cabbage to a serving dish. Stir in the bacon. Serve hot.

Makes 8 servings
8 minutes at high pressure

tuscan **green beans** with pancetta and olives

Green beans don't always need to be cooked tender-crisp—well-done beans have a lot of flavor, too. These boldly seasoned beans are perfect with simply grilled chicken or steak. If you have flat Italian-style (sometimes called Romano) green beans, this recipe will be even tastier.

1 tablespoon extra-virgin olive oil

2 ounces pancetta, coarsely chopped (see Note)

1 small onion, chopped

3 garlic cloves, minced

1 pound green beans, trimmed, cut into 1½-inch lengths

½ cup water

2 teaspoons chopped fresh sage or 1 teaspoon dried sage

⅛ teaspoon salt, plus more to taste

⅛ teaspoon freshly ground black pepper, plus more to taste

⅓ cup black Mediterranean olives, pitted and coarsely chopped

1. In a 5- to 7-quart pressure cooker, heat the oil over medium heat. Add the pancetta and cook, stirring occasionally, until it renders most of its fat and is browned, about 5 minutes. Add the onion and garlic and cook until beginning to soften, about 1 minute. Stir in the green beans, water, sage, ⅛ teaspoon salt, and ⅛ teaspoon pepper.

2. Lock the lid in place. Bring to high pressure over high heat. Adjust the heat to maintain pressure. Cook for 2 minutes. Remove from the heat and quick-release the pressure. Open the lid, tilting it away from you to block any escaping steam.

3. Using a slotted spoon, transfer the green beans to a warm serving dish and cover with foil to keep warm. Add the olives to the pot. Bring to a boil, uncovered, over high heat. Cook until the liquid is evaporated to about ⅓ cup, about 2 minutes. Pour over the green beans and mix. Serve with additional salt and pepper. Serve hot.

Note: Pancetta, unsmoked bacon, can be found at most Italian delicatessens. If necessary, use regular sliced bacon, but simmer uncovered in water to cover for 3 minutes to remove some of the smoky flavor.

———————————

Makes 4 to 6 servings
2 minutes on high pressure

scalloped **cauliflower** and mushrooms

Cauliflower in cheese sauce may sound like a somewhat common dish, but this version gets a lift from leeks and dried porcini mushrooms. It's made in the pressure cooker, then run under the broiler to give it a nice finish. Serve alongside grilled fish fillets, or as a vegetarian main course.

3 tablespoons unsalted butter, plus more for the dish

1 cup chopped leeks, white and pale green parts only (3 medium leeks)

½ ounce dried porcini mushrooms, quickly rinsed under cold water and coarsely chopped

1 large (2½ pounds) head cauliflower, trimmed and cut into florets about 1½ inches across

1 cup Homemade Chicken Stock (page 23), canned low-sodium broth, or water

⅛ teaspoon salt, plus more to taste

⅛ teaspoon freshly ground white pepper, plus more to taste

2 tablespoons cornstarch

2 cups half-and-half or milk

1 cup shredded Gruyère or Swiss cheese

2 tablespoons freshly grated Parmesan cheese

1. Position a rack 6 inches from the source of heat and preheat the broiler. Lightly butter a 9 x 13-inch flameproof dish.

2. In a 5- to 7-quart pressure cooker, melt 2 tablespoons butter over medium heat. Add the leeks and dried mushrooms and cook until the leeks soften, about 1 minute. Add the cauliflower, stock, ⅛ teaspoon salt, and ⅛ teaspoon pepper.

3. Lock the lid in place. Bring to high pressure over high heat. Adjust the heat to maintain the pressure. Cook for 30 seconds. Remove from the heat and quick-release the pressure. Open the lid, tilting it away from you to block any escaping steam. Using a slotted spoon, transfer the cauliflower to the prepared dish. Cover with foil to keep warm and set aside. Return the uncovered pot to medium heat and bring to a boil.

4. In a small bowl, sprinkle the cornstarch over the half-and-half and whisk until dissolved. Whisk into the pot and cook until thickened. Remove from the heat and stir in the Gruyère cheese until smooth. Season with additional salt and pepper. Pour over the cauliflower. Sprinkle with the Parmesan cheese and dot with the remaining 1 tablespoon butter.

5. Broil until the top is lightly browned, 1 to 2 minutes. Serve hot.

———

Makes 6 to 8 servings
30 seconds at high pressure

collard greens with smoked turkey

Until recently, most southerners used a ham hock to "season" their greens, which were long-simmered to mellow their bitterness. Now, many experienced cooks we know use smoked turkey wings instead to lend a ham-like flavor without a lot of cholesterol. The pressure-cooked version begins by making a spicy broth from the wings, then adding the greens. While smoked turkey wings (and necks and tails) are a staple at groceries with a multiethnic clientele, if you can't find them, substitute a smoked ham hock, and pressure-cook it for 20 minutes.

2½ pounds collard greens
1 tablespoon vegetable oil
1 medium onion, chopped
4 garlic cloves, minced
2 small (about 1¼ pounds total) smoked turkey wings, chopped into 2-inch pieces (if necessary, ask the butcher to do this)
2 cups water
½ teaspoon crushed hot red pepper flakes
¾ teaspoon salt

1. Remove the tough stems from the greens and discard. Fill a sink with lukewarm water. Place the leaves in the water and agitate them well to loosen any grit (which is loosened more easily by tepid than cold water). Lift the greens from the water and set aside to drain. Coarsely chop the greens.

2. In a 5- to 7-quart pressure cooker, heat the oil over medium heat. Add the onion and garlic and cook until the onion begins to soften, about 1 minute. Add the turkey wings, water, hot pepper, and salt. Lock the lid in place. Bring to high pressure over high heat. Adjust the heat to maintain the pressure. Cook for 10 minutes.

3. Remove from the heat and quick-release the pressure. Open the lid, tilting it away from you to block any escaping steam. Return the uncovered pot to medium-high heat and bring the cooking liquid to a boil. In batches, stir the greens, letting the first batch wilt before adding another. The greens should not fill the cooker more than halfway.

4. Replace the lid and lock in place. Return to high pressure over high heat. Adjust the heat to maintain high pressure. Cook for 5 minutes. Remove from the heat and quick-release the pressure. Open the lid. Drain the greens in a colander, reserving the "cooking liquor," if desired. Pick out and discard any loose turkey bones. (The liquor, dipped into cornbread or sipped on its own, is considered a delicacy by discriminating southern cooks.) Serve the greens immediately.

Makes 6 servings
10 minutes at high pressure for the turkey,
then 5 minutes at high pressure for the greens

VEGETABLES

jalapeño and cheese corn pudding

Corn pudding is a family favorite. This zesty version is easy to make in a pressure cooker, freeing up the oven for the main course.

Butter, for the dish
One 14¾-ounce can cream-style corn
⅓ cup all-purpose flour
1 tablespoon sugar
½ teaspoon baking powder
1 garlic clove, crushed through a garlic press
¼ teaspoon salt
¼ teaspoon freshly ground black pepper
3 large eggs plus 1 large egg yolk
½ cup heavy cream
½ cup shredded sharp Cheddar cheese
1 jalapeño pepper, seeded and minced

1. Lightly butter a 1½-quart soufflé dish. In a medium bowl, whisk together the corn, flour, sugar, baking powder, garlic, salt, and pepper. In another medium bowl, whisk the eggs and egg yolk and cream until blended. Whisk into the corn mixture, just until combined. Stir in all but 1 tablespoon of the cheese and the jalapeño. Pour into the prepared dish. Sprinkle with the reserved tablespoon of cheese. Butter a 12-inch-long piece of heavy-duty aluminum foil. Tightly cover the dish with the foil, buttered side down (the foil should come down the sides of the dish).

2. Place the trivet in the bottom of a 5- to 7-quart pressure cooker. Pour 2 cups of water into the pot. Center the covered dish in an aluminum foil "cradle" (see page 145). Using the cradle, lower the dish onto the trivet.

3. Lock the lid in place. Bring to high pressure over high heat. Adjust the heat to maintain pressure. Cook for 28 minutes. Remove from the heat. Allow the pressure to drop naturally for 7 minutes. Quick-release the remaining pressure in the pot.

4. Open the lid, tilting it away from you to block any escaping steam. Using the cradle, lift the dish out of the pot. Let stand for 2 or 3 minutes. Remove the foil. If necessary, using paper towels, blot any water on the surface of the pudding. Sprinkle with the remaining 1 tablespoon of cheese, and serve hot.

Makes 4 to 6 servings
28 minutes at high pressure

steamed **potatoes** with **dill butter**

Steamed potatoes have a lovely simplicity that makes them a favorite side dish. To make them in a pressure cooker, slice them first—whole potatoes have a tendency to split. Medium-sized potatoes cook more evenly than large ones.

2½ pounds medium red-skinned potatoes, peeled
  and cut into ¼-inch-thick rounds
Salt, to taste
3 tablespoons unsalted butter
2 tablespoons chopped fresh dill
Freshly ground black pepper, to taste

1. Place a collapsible aluminum steamer in a 5- to 7-quart pressure cooker (the steamer holds more potatoes than the typical steamer basket that comes with most cookers). Add the minimum amount of water as required by your cooker to bring up to pressure. This could be anywhere from ½ cup to 1½ cups, but do not let the water touch the bottom of the steamer. Place the potatoes in the steamer, seasoning them lightly with salt. Lock the lid in place. Bring to high pressure over high heat. Adjust the heat to maintain pressure. Cook for 2 minutes, 45 seconds. Remove from the heat and quick-release the pressure. Open the lid, tilting it away from you to block any escaping steam. Using the tip of a small sharp knife, check the potatoes for tenderness. If necessary, cover the pot with the lid (do not lock) and steam the potatoes over medium heat until tender.

2. Transfer the potatoes to a medium bowl. Add the butter and dill and toss. Season with pepper and salt. Serve immediately.

———

Makes 4 to 6 servings
2 minutes, 45 seconds at high pressure

quick **garlic** mashed **potatoes**

Mashed potatoes in less than 15 minutes from start to finish?!

3 pounds medium Idaho or russet potatoes,
   peeled and cut into ½-inch slices
4 cups water
8 large garlic cloves, crushed under a knife and
   peeled
½ teaspoon salt, plus more to taste
½ cup hot milk
3 tablespoons unsalted butter
¼ teaspoon freshly ground black pepper

1. In a 5- to 7-quart pressure cooker, combine the potatoes, water, garlic, and ½ teaspoon salt. Lock the lid in place. Bring to high pressure over high heat. Cook for 5 minutes. Remove from the heat and quick-release the pressure. Open the lid, tilting it way from you to block any escaping steam. Drain well.

2. Return the potatoes and garlic to the warm cooker. Using an electric hand mixer or a potato masher, mash the potatoes with the milk and butter. Season with additional salt and the pepper. Serve hot.

Makes 4 servings
5 minutes at high pressure

potato salad with mustard and herbs

Here's Arlene's potato salad *à la française,* with bright and fresh flavors. It's a good choice for a warm summer salad because it won't spoil as quickly as mayonnaise-based versions. There are a few tricks to getting the potatoes cooked into firm, yet tender, slices. Use a collapsible aluminum steamer to hold the potatoes in the pot so they aren't submerged in water. Be sure to use waxy-fleshed red or white potatoes—they will hold their shape better than starchy russets or Idaho potatoes. And don't cut them too thin, or they'll fall apart. It is better to err on the thick side and have to steam undercooked slices for a few extra minutes than have mushy, crumbled potatoes.

2½ pounds medium red-skinned potatoes, peeled and cut into ¼-inch-thick rounds
3 tablespoons dry white wine or dry vermouth
½ teaspoon salt, plus more to taste
2 tablespoons white wine vinegar
1 tablespoon Dijon mustard
⅓ cup olive oil
1 tablespoon finely chopped fresh rosemary
1 tablespoon finely chopped fresh chives
Freshly ground black pepper, to taste

1. Place a collapsible aluminum steamer in a 5- to 7-quart pressure cooker (the steamer holds more potatoes than the typical steamer basket that comes with most cookers). Add the minimum amount of water as required by your cooker to bring up to pressure. This could be anywhere from ½ cup to 1½ cups, but do not let the water touch the bottom of the steamer. Place the potatoes in the steamer. Lock the lid in place. Bring to high pressure over high heat. Adjust the heat to maintain pressure. Cook for 2 minutes, 45 seconds. Remove from the heat and quick-release the pressure. Open the lid, tilting it away from you to block any escaping steam. Using the tip of a small sharp knife, check the potatoes for tenderness. If necessary, cover the pot with the lid (do not lock) and steam the potatoes over medium heat until tender.

2. Transfer the potatoes to a medium bowl. Toss with the wine and ½ teaspoon salt, taking care not to break up the slices too much. In a small bowl, whisk together the vinegar and mustard. Gradually whisk in the oil. Stir in the rosemary and chives. Fold into the potatoes. Season with pepper and additional salt. Serve warm or cooled to room temperature, but not chilled.

Makes 4 to 6 servings
2 minutes, 45 seconds at high pressure

orange-glazed yams

Sweet candied yams are a holiday menu staple. They can be stubborn and often take quite awhile to cook through, but not when a pressure cooker is around. Because they're rich, three yams will probably suffice for six to eight servings. Use orange-fleshed Louisiana yams, not pale yellow sweet potatoes (they're actually quite different, and the Louisiana yams are much sweeter). It's important to choose long, narrow yams, which will cook more evenly than large, round ones.

½ cup fresh orange juice
½ cup water (or more to meet your cooker's minimum liquid requirement)
3 medium (10 ounces each) Louisiana yams, preferably with long, narrow shapes, peeled and cut lengthwise
⅓ cup packed light brown sugar
Grated zest of ½ orange
⅛ teaspoon salt
2 tablespoons unsalted butter, in small pieces

1. Pour the orange juice and water into a 5- to 7-quart pressure cooker. Fit with the steamer basket. Stack the yams in the basket, sprinkling with the brown sugar, orange zest, and salt, and dotting with the butter.

2. Lock the lid in place. Bring to high pressure over high heat. Adjust the heat to maintain the pressure. Cook for 7 minutes. Remove from the heat and quick-release the pressure. Open the lid, tilting it away from you to block any escaping steam. Using the tip of a small sharp knife, check the yams for tenderness. If necessary, cover the pot with the lid (do not lock) and steam the yams over medium heat until tender. Using a slotted spatula or spoon, transfer the yams to a warmed serving dish, and cover with foil to keep warm.

3. Return the uncovered pot to high heat and bring the cooking liquid to a boil. Boil until thickened, 3 to 5 minutes (about 10 minutes if more than ½ cup water was used). Using a small knife, cut the yams into chunks. Pour the glaze over the yams and serve hot.

Makes 6 to 8 servings
7 minutes at high pressure

VEGETABLES

cauliflower and carrot curry

This recipe, adapted from Rick's book *On Rice*, makes an almost instant vegetarian dinner. It is great spooned over basmati rice. Madras-style curry powder is a mild blend, and the one most likely to be found in supermarkets. If you buy your curry powder at a spice shop, be sure it is not too hot for your taste.

1 tablespoon vegetable oil
4 medium carrots, cut into ½-inch-thick rounds
1 large onion, chopped
1 garlic clove, finely chopped
2 teaspoons Madras-style curry powder
½ teaspoon ground cumin
¼ teaspoon salt
1 medium (1¾ pounds) cauliflower, broken into 1½-inch florets
1 cup Homemade Vegetable Stock (page 26), canned vegetable broth, or low-sodium chicken broth
½ cup canned unsweetened coconut milk
1 teaspoon cornstarch
1 tablespoon water
1 cup thawed frozen petite peas
6 cups hot cooked rice, for serving (2 cups raw rice)
Chopped fresh cilantro, for garnish (optional)

1. In a 5- to 7-quart pressure cooker, heat the oil over medium-high heat. Add the carrots, onion, and garlic. Cook, stirring often, until the onion begins to soften, about 2 minutes. Add the curry, cumin, and salt and stir until fragrant, about 20 seconds. Add the cauliflower, stock, and coconut milk.

2. Lock the lid in place. Bring to high pressure over high heat. Adjust the heat to maintain the pressure. Cook for 1 minute. Remove from the heat and quick-release the pressure. Open the lid, tilting it away from you to block any escaping steam.

3. In a small bowl, sprinkle the cornstarch over the water and stir to dissolve. Stir the dissolved cornstarch and peas into the cooking liquid. Bring to a boil—the sauce will be lightly thickened. Serve immediately, spooned over the rice, sprinkling with cilantro, if desired.

Makes 4 to 6 servings
1 minute at high pressure

moroccan vegetable stew with sweet spices and raisins

Moroccan cooks love the interplay of sweet flavors with savory ones. The natural sweetness of butternut squash, carrots, and raisins is tempered by the spices and lemon juice. Spoon the stew over couscous or rice.

2 tablespoons olive oil
1 medium onion, chopped
2 medium carrots, cut into ½-inch-thick rounds
2 garlic cloves, minced
½ teaspoon paprika, preferably sweet Hungarian
½ teaspoon ground cumin
¼ teaspoon ground cinnamon
¼ teaspoon salt
⅛ teaspoon ground hot red pepper flakes
One small (1¾ pounds) butternut squash, peeled, seeded, and cut into 1-inch pieces
One 14½-ounce can tomatoes in juice, drained and chopped
½ cup Homemade Vegetable Stock (page 26), canned vegetable broth, or low-sodium chicken broth
½ cup raisins
2 tablespoons fresh lemon juice
1 teaspoon sugar
Hot cooked couscous, for serving

1. In a 5- to 7-quart pressure cooker, heat the oil over medium-high heat. Add the onion, carrots, and garlic. Cook, stirring often, until the vegetables soften, about 2 minutes. Add the paprika, cumin, cinnamon, salt, and hot pepper and stir until fragrant, about 20 seconds. Stir in the squash, tomatoes, and stock.

2. Lock the lid in place. Bring to high pressure over high heat. Adjust the heat to maintain the pressure. Cook for 3 minutes. Remove from the heat and quick-release the pressure. Open the lid, tilting it away from you to block any escaping steam. Stir in the raisins, lemon juice, and sugar. Let stand for 2 minutes.

3. Serve hot, spooned over the couscous.

Makes 4 to 6 servings
3 minutes at high pressure

caponata

It may not seem like you really need two quarts of Arlene's caponata, the sweet-and-sour Sicilian eggplant spread, but it will disappear quickly. It is well known as a piquant dip for pita bread and sliced, toasted Italian bread. But it can also be served as a condiment for grilled fish and meats, spread on crusty bread as a sandwich filling, or tossed with spaghetti for a quick sauce (the last is especially good with the addition of drained canned tuna or finely chopped anchovies).

⅓ cup pine nuts
½ cup olive oil
2 medium onions, chopped
4 medium celery ribs with leaves, cut into ¼-inch slices
1 medium (1½ pounds) eggplant, cut into ¾-inch cubes
One 28-ounce can crushed tomatoes
12 ounces Mediterranean green olives, pitted and chopped
1 cup golden raisins
7 tablespoons balsamic vinegar
3 tablespoons red wine vinegar
3 tablespoons sugar
3 tablespoons bottled capers, rinsed and drained
½ teaspoon salt, plus more to taste
¼ teaspoon crushed hot red pepper flakes

1. Heat a medium skillet over medium heat. Add the pine nuts and cook, stirring almost constantly, until light brown. Transfer to a plate and set aside.

2. In a 5- to 7-quart pressure cooker, heat the oil over medium heat. Add the onions and celery and cook, stirring occasionally, until the vegetables begin to soften, about 2 minutes. Add the eggplant, toma- toes, olives, raisins, balsamic and wine vinegars, sugar, capers, ½ teaspoon salt, and hot pepper. Mix well. Lock the lid in place. Bring to high pressure over high heat. Adjust the heat to maintain the pressure. Cook for 8 minutes. Remove from the heat and quick- release the pressure. Open the lid, tilting it away from you to block any escaping steam. Transfer to a bowl and cool completely. Stir in the toasted pine nuts.

3. Cover tightly and refrigerate overnight. (The caponata can be refrigerated, stored in airtight con- tainers, for up to 10 days.) Bring to room temperature and season with additional salt, if needed, before serving.

Makes about 2 quarts
8 minutes at high pressure

beet and orange salad

One of the most refreshing first-course salads around, this gives a bright note of color to a winter menu. Try to buy beets with the greens attached, as the greens are delicious. If they are young and tender, tear them up and add to a green salad (but not too many, as they have a mild bitterness that can overwhelm sweet lettuce). If older, add them to the Collard Greens with Smoked Turkey (page 134).

4 medium (about 4 ounces each) beets
3 large seedless oranges
3 tablespoons balsamic vinegar
½ teaspoon salt
¼ teaspoon freshly ground black pepper
½ cup extra-virgin olive oil
2 tablespoons finely chopped shallots
2 ounces firm goat cheese, such as Bucheron, crumbled

1. If the beets have their greens attached, cut them off, leaving about 1 inch of the stems attached to the beets (this helps the beets keep their color during cooking). Scrub the beets under cold running water, but do not peel.

2. Fit a 5- to 7-quart pressure cooker with the steamer basket. Pour 2 cups water into the cooker. Place the beets in the basket. Lock the lid in place. Bring to high pressure over high heat. Adjust the heat to maintain the pressure. Cook for 18 minutes. Remove from the heat and quick-release the pressure. Open the lid, tilting it away from you to block any escaping steam. Cool the beets completely. Slip off the skins and slice into ¼-inch-thick slices.

3. Grate the zest from 1 orange and set aside. Using a serrated knife, cut off the skin from all the oranges. Cut the oranges into ½-inch-thick rounds. Arrange the beets and oranges in overlapping rows on a serving platter.

4. In a small bowl, whisk the vinegar, orange zest, salt, and pepper. Gradually whisk in the oil. Stir in the shallots. Pour over the beets and oranges and cover tightly. Refrigerate to blend the flavors, at least 1 and up to 6 hours.

5. If chilled, let stand at room temperature for 30 minutes before serving. Top with the cheese and serve immediately.

Makes 4 to 6 servings
18 minutes at high pressure

desserts and fruits

What a pleasure it is to serve a wonderful dessert in the middle of the summer without having to turn on the oven! Pressure-cooked cheesecakes are so moist and creamy, we rarely make them in the oven anymore. Custards from the pressure cooker turn out so silky-smooth that our pastry chef friends ask for our secret recipe. We love telling them that it's not a secret recipe, but a "secret" cooking appliance. With the pressure cooker, you can prepare elegant, light fruit desserts like Riesling-poached pears and dried fruit compote in a few minutes.

Some pressure-cooked desserts use special pans or containers, which you may already have in your kitchen. You'll need a 7-inch springform pan for cheesecakes, a 1½-quart soufflé dish for bread puddings, and 4- to 5-ounce custard cups or ramekins for custards. All are easily available at kitchenware stores and by mail order from Adventures in Cooking, Wayne, NJ (adventuresincooking.com).

Getting a springform pan or soufflé dish in and out of a pressure cooker may seem awkward, but an aluminum foil "cradle" makes it easy: Tear off a 24-inch length of aluminum foil. Fold the strip lengthwise in half, then in half again, to make a sturdy strip of foil about 3 inches wide. Place the strip on a work surface. Place the pan or soufflé dish in the center of the strip, and bring up the ends. Using the ends as a handle, the dessert can be lifted in and out of the pot. Fold the foil handles down over the dessert when closing the cooker.

tips for **desserts**

➤ When covering cooking containers for pressure cooking, use heavy-duty aluminum foil—it keeps out moisture better than regular foil.

➤ If you plan to do a lot of dessert-making in your cooker, store the foil strip with the pot to use again.

➤ Sometimes a puddle of water will form on the cheesecake top or custard. Simply lay a piece of paper towel over the water to blot it up.

➤ Bread puddings are best when prepared from firm-textured day-old bread. Let the bread stand at room temperature overnight, uncovered. Or, cut up the bread and bake in a preheated 350°F oven for 10 minutes. Do not toast the bread. The bread will firm as it cools.

➤ Try to serve your bread puddings warm—they're really luscious this way. If you wish, make the bread pudding up to 1 day ahead and refrigerate. When ready to serve, cover with microwave-safe wrap and microwave at medium until warmed through, about 2 minutes.

➤ Why do pressure cookers make such wonderfully smooth custards? Eggs break down into solids and liquids at temperatures above 325°F, and the pressure cooker's internal temperature is only 250°F. Because of the moderate temperature and moist cooking atmosphere, the custards won't get a skin on top, either.

chocolate pots de crème

These elegant, intensely chocolate custards will finish off a meal with a few rich, satisfying bites. Use a high-quality bittersweet chocolate for the best results.

1 cup half-and-half
½ cup plus 2 teaspoons sugar
2 ounces bittersweet chocolate, finely chopped
1 large egg plus 2 large egg yolks
¼ teaspoon vanilla
½ cup heavy cream

1. In a medium saucepan, bring the half-and-half and ½ cup sugar to a simmer over medium heat, stirring often to dissolve the sugar. Remove from the heat and add the chocolate. Let stand 1 minute, then whisk to melt the chocolate.

2. In a medium bowl, whisk the egg, egg yolks, and vanilla to combine. Gradually whisk in the hot cream mixture. Strain through a wire sieve into a large glass measuring cup, and pour evenly into four ½-cup ramekins or custard cups. Cover each ramekin tightly with aluminum foil.

3. Place the trivet and steamer basket in a 5- to 7-quart pressure cooker. Pour 2 cups water into the cooker. Stack the cups, pyramid-style, in the cooker. Lock the lid in place. Bring to high pressure over high heat. Adjust the heat to maintain the pressure. Cook for 8 minutes. Remove from the heat and quick-release the pressure. Open the lid, tilting it away from you to block any escaping steam. Let the custards stand in the pot for 3 minutes for easier handling. Using kitchen tongs, remove the cups from the cooker. Remove the foil. The centers should wobble slightly—they will set as they cool. Cool the custards to room temperature. Cover each with plastic wrap and refrigerate until chilled, at least 4 hours.

4. In a chilled small bowl, beat the cream with the remaining 2 teaspoons sugar until thickened. Top each pot de crème with a dollop of whipped cream and serve chilled.

Makes 4 servings
8 minutes at high pressure

orange and chocolate marble cheesecake

Serve this cheesecake with fresh strawberries and raspberries for a summertime treat. Use a light dusting of chocolate cookie crumbs, as a thicker crust could overpower the rich filling.

2 tablespoons unsalted butter, melted
¼ cup chocolate wafer or chocolate-flavored graham cracker crumbs
3 ounces bittersweet or semisweet chocolate, finely chopped
1 pound cream cheese, at room temperature
¾ cup sugar
½ cup sour cream
3 tablespoons all-purpose flour
2 teaspoons vanilla extract
Grated zest of 1 orange
3 large eggs plus 1 large egg yolk
Softened butter, for the foil

1. Wrap the bottom of a 7-inch springform pan tightly with heavy-duty aluminum foil. Butter the inside of the pan with all of the melted butter. Sprinkle the bottom of the pan with the cookie crumbs.

2. In the top part of a double boiler over hot, not simmering, water, melt the chocolate, stirring occasionally, until smooth. Remove the top part of the double boiler from the heat and let the chocolate cool until tepid.

3. In a medium bowl, using a hand-held electric mixer set at medium speed, beat the cream cheese and sugar until smooth. Beat in the sour cream, flour, vanilla, and orange zest. Beat in the eggs and egg yolk.

4. Pour about one-fourth of the cheese mixture into the prepared pan. Pour another one-fourth of the mixture into a small bowl and set aside. Stir the cooled chocolate into the remaining cheese mixture until well blended. Pour over the vanilla layer in the pan. Pour the remaining vanilla mixture over the chocolate mixture in a swirl pattern. Run a knife through the two mixtures together to make a marble pattern. Butter a 15-inch-long piece of aluminum foil. Tightly cover the pan with the foil, buttered side down, allowing some room for expansion at the top for the cheesecake to rise. (The foil should completely cover the pan.)

5. Place the trivet in the bottom of a 5- to 7-quart pressure cooker. Pour 2 cups of water into the pot. Center the covered dish in an aluminum foil "cradle" (see page 145). Using the cradle, lower the dish onto the trivet.

6. Lock the lid in place. Bring to high pressure over high heat. Adjust the heat to maintain the pressure. Cook for 25 minutes. Remove from the heat. Allow the pressure to drop naturally, about 20 minutes. Open the lid, tilting it away from you to block any escaping steam.

7. Using the cradle, lift the dish out of the pot. Let stand for 2 or 3 minutes. Remove the foil. If necessary, using paper towels, blot any water on the surface of the cheesecake. Run a sharp knife around the inside of the pan to release the cheesecake from the sides. Place on a wire cake rack and cool completely.

8. Remove the sides of the pan. Cover the cheesecake with plastic wrap and refrigerate until well chilled, at least 4 hours. Serve chilled, using a sharp knife dipped into hot water to cut each slice.

Makes 6 to 8 servings
25 minutes at high pressure

apricot cheesecake

Fresh apricots are a summertime treat, but dried apricots have a more intense flavor that makes them perfect for baking. The filling should be prepared in a food processor to purée the apricots. Otherwise, press the softened apricots through a wire sieve and make the filling with an electric mixer, adding the apricot purée with the eggs.

2 tablespoons unsalted butter, melted
¼ cup crushed amaretti cookies, or use any crisp cookie
8 ounces dried apricots, cut into ¼-inch-wide slices
½ cup water
1 pound cream cheese, at room temperature
¾ cup sugar
¼ cup sour cream, at room temperature
2 tablespoons cornstarch
3 large eggs plus 1 large egg yolk, at room temperature
¼ teaspoon vanilla extract
Softened butter, for the foil
¼ cup apricot preserves

1. Wrap the bottom of a 7-inch springform pan tightly with heavy-duty aluminum foil. Butter the inside of the pan with all of the melted butter. Sprinkle the bottom of the pan with the cookie crumbs.

2. In a 5- to 7-quart pressure cooker, combine the apricots and water. Bring to high pressure over high heat. Adjust the heat to maintain the pressure. Cook for 30 seconds. Remove from the heat and quick-release the pressure. Open the lid, tilting it away from you to block any escaping steam. Drain the mixture in a wire sieve set over a medium bowl; reserve the liquid. Transfer 3 tablespoons of the apricots to a food processor fitted with the metal blade. Set the remaining apricots aside.

3. Add the cream cheese and sugar to the food processor. Process until smooth, stopping the machine occasionally to scrape down the sides of the bowl. Add the sour cream and cornstarch and pulse until combined. With the machine running, add the eggs, one at a time, then the yolk and vanilla, scraping down the bowl as needed. Spread evenly in the prepared pan.

4. Butter a 15-inch-long piece of aluminum foil. Tightly cover the pan with the foil, buttered side down, allowing some room for expansion at the top for the cheesecake to rise. (The foil should completely cover the pan.)

5. Place the trivet in the bottom of the pot. Pour 2 cups of water into the pot. Center the covered dish in an aluminum foil "cradle" (see page 145). Using the cradle, lower the pan onto the trivet.

6. Lock the lid in place. Bring to high pressure over high heat. Adjust the heat to maintain the pressure. Cook for 25 minutes. Remove from the heat. Allow the pressure to drop naturally, about 20 minutes. Open the lid, tilting it away from you to block any escaping steam.

7. Using the cradle, lift the pan out of the pot. Let stand for 2 or 3 minutes. Remove the foil. If necessary, blot any water on the surface of the cheesecake with a paper towel. Run a sharp knife around the inside of the pan to release the cheesecake from the

sides. Place on a wire cake rack and cool completely.

8. Remove the sides of the pan. Cover the cheese-cake with plastic wrap and refrigerate until well chilled, at least 4 hours.

9. To make the glaze, in a medium saucepan, combine the apricot preserves, reserved apricots, and 3 tablespoons of the apricot cooking liquid. Bring to a boil over medium heat and stir until slightly thick-ened, about 1 minute. Place the cheesecake on a serv-ing plate. Spread the apricot glaze over the top of the cheesecake, letting a little of the glaze drip down the sides. Let stand at room temperature for about 30 minutes. Serve, using a sharp knife dipped into hot water to cut each slice.

Makes 6 to 8 servings
25 minutes at high pressure

café con leche flan

If you need convincing that pressure cookers do an incredible job of preparing silky-smooth custards, make these coffee-flavored flans—the proof is in the pudding.

Butter, for the ramekins
½ cup plus ⅓ cup sugar
2 tablespoons cold water
1½ teaspoons instant espresso powder (see Note)
2 teaspoons boiling water
2 large eggs, at room temperature
1 cup half-and-half, heated until simmering
½ teaspoon vanilla
Pinch of ground cinnamon (optional)

1. Lightly butter four ½-cup ramekins or custard cups and set aside.

2. Place ½ cup sugar in a medium saucepan and sprinkle with the 2 tablespoons cold water. Cook over medium-high heat, stirring constantly, just until the mixture is boiling. Cook without stirring, occasionally swirling the saucepan by the handle to combine the darker syrup at the edges with the clear syrup in the center, until the caramel is evenly golden brown, about 3 minutes. Immediately pour equal amounts of the hot caramel into the prepared cups. Quickly tilt each cup to partially coat the inside with caramel.

3. In a small bowl, dissolve the espresso powder in the boiling water. In a medium bowl, whisk the eggs and the remaining ⅓ cup sugar. Gradually whisk in the hot half-and-half, then the dissolved espresso, vanilla, and cinnamon, if desired. Strain the custard mixture through a fine wire sieve into a large glass measuring cup to remove any bits of egg white, and divide evenly among the cups. Cover each cup tightly with aluminum foil.

4. Place the trivet and steamer basket in a 5- to 7-quart pressure cooker. Pour 2 cups water into the cooker. Stack the cups, pyramid-style, in the cooker. Lock the lid in place. Bring to high pressure over high heat. Adjust the heat to maintain the pressure. Cook for 8 minutes. Remove from the heat and quick-release the pressure. Open the lid, tilting it away from you to block any escaping steam. Let the flans stand in the cooker for about 3 minutes to cool.

5. Using kitchen tongs, remove the cups from the cooker. Remove the foil. The centers of the flans should be very slightly underdone and wobble when shaken. If necessary, re-cover with foil, return to the cooker, and cook at high pressure for an additional 1 minute. If there is a small puddle of water on the surface of a flan, carefully blot it with a paper towel.

6. Cool the flans to room temperature. Cover each with plastic wrap and refrigerate until chilled, at least 4 hours.

7. To serve, run a sharp, thin knife around the inside of each cup to release the flan. One at a time, invert the flans onto a serving plate. Hold the cup onto the plate and give a sharp shake to unmold the flan and its caramel syrup.

Note: Instant espresso powder is available at Italian grocers and specialty food stores. If unavailable, substitute 2 teaspoons regular instant coffee.

Makes 4 servings
8 minutes at high pressure

caramel knowledge

Making the caramel for the self-contained sauce in a flan or crème caramel is very simple, but here are some tips to side-step any mistakes.

➤ Have the custard cups buttered and ready, and pour in the hot caramel without delay, as it will thicken quickly as it cools.

➤ Don't stir the sugar syrup after it comes to a boil—that encourages crystallization. If you want to mix the syrup, swirl the pot by its handle.

➤ With this caramel, you can ignore any crystals that form inside the pan. If you prefer, you may use a pastry brush dipped in hot water, pressing hard against the side of the pan, to wash them down into the boiling syrup.

➤ To check the caramel for doneness, you do not need a candy thermometer—use your eyes and nose. The darker the caramel, the deeper the flavor. It should look golden brown and have a distinct, sharp aroma that seems on the verge of burning.

ginger crème brûlée

When the culinary history of the late twentieth century is written, surely crème brûlée will emerge as one of our era's favorites. This version gets an added fillip from crystallized ginger, available at Asian markets, specialty stores, and many supermarkets. Two tips: The brown sugar topping will melt more evenly if the sugar is allowed to stand uncovered at room temperature for a few hours or overnight to dry it out. And placing the ramekins in a pan of ice cubes keeps the custard chilled while the sugar melts in the broiler.

1½ cups heavy cream
4 large egg yolks
¼ cup granulated sugar
½ teaspoon vanilla extract
3 tablespoons finely chopped crystallized ginger
3 tablespoons packed light brown sugar

1. In a small saucepan over medium heat, bring the cream to a simmer. In a medium bowl, whisk the yolks, sugar, and vanilla to combine. Gradually whisk in the hot cream. Strain through a wire sieve into a large glass measuring cup, and pour evenly into four ½-cup ramekins or custard cups. Divide the ginger evenly among the ramekins. Cover each ramekin tightly with aluminum foil.

2. Place the trivet and steamer basket in a 5- to 7-quart pressure cooker. Pour 2 cups water into the cooker. Stack the cups, pyramid-style, in the cooker. Lock the lid in place. Bring to high pressure over high heat. Adjust the heat to maintain the pressure. Cook for 8 minutes. Remove from the heat and quick-release the pressure. Open the lid, tilting it away from you to block any escaping steam. Let the custards stand in the pot for 3 minutes for easier handling. Using kitchen tongs, remove the cups from the cooker. Remove the foil. The centers should wobble slightly—they will set as they cool. If necessary, recover with foil, return to the cooker, and cook for an additional 1 minute at high pressure. Cool the custards to room temperature. Cover each with plastic wrap and refrigerate until chilled, at least 4 hours.

3. When ready to serve, position a broiler rack about 6 inches from the source of heat and preheat the broiler. Unwrap the custards. Rub the brown sugar through a small wire sieve, coating the top of each custard with a layer of sugar. Place the ramekins in a baking pan, and surround them with ice cubes.

4. Broil the custards, watching carefully to avoid scorching, until the sugar melts, 1 to 2 minutes. Remove the ramekins from the baking pan and serve immediately.

Makes 4 servings
8 minutes at high pressure

creamy rice pudding

In Europe, many cooks simmer their rice pudding on the stove, making a firm pudding that doesn't need any eggs to add richness. This pressure-cooked version of the method is best cooked on low pressure to avoid scorching the milk and sugar, but see the Note following the recipe if your cooker has only one setting. Use a medium-grain rice that has plenty of starch. Possibilities include Latino brands (such as Goya) or imported Italian or Spanish varieties (Arborio, Baldo, Carnaroli, Vialone Nano, Valencia, or "paella" rice). Personalize the pudding to suit your taste. Leave out the cinnamon, or substitute dried cranberries or cherries for the raisins and orange for the lemon zest.

4 cups milk, plus more as needed
1½ cups medium-grain rice (do not rinse)
1 cup sugar
Grated zest of 1 lemon
½ teaspoon salt
½ cup raisins or golden raisins
2 teaspoons vanilla extract
¼ teaspoon ground cinnamon
Approximately 1½ cups heavy cream, half-and-half, or milk, for serving

1. In a 5- to 7-quart pressure cooker, mix the 4 cups milk with the rice, sugar, lemon zest, and salt.

2. Lock the lid in place. Bring to low pressure over high heat. (See Note.) Adjust the heat to maintain the pressure. Cook for 11 minutes. Remove from the heat. Quick-release the pressure. Open the lid, tilting it away from you to block any escaping steam. If the rice isn't tender, replace the lid (no need to lock it) and let stand for 10 to 15 minutes, allowing the residual heat to continue cooking the rice. Do not return to the heat. Add the raisins, vanilla, and cinnamon and stir well. If serving warm, transfer to a serving dish. If desired, cool the pudding, cover, and refrigerate until chilled, at least 2 hours. Whether warm or chilled, if the pudding seems too firm, stir in enough additional milk to reach the desired consistency.

3. Serve the pudding in bowls, topping each serving with a few tablespoons of cream or milk.

Note: If you have only a high-pressure setting on your cooker, butter the inside of the cooker. Cook the rice mixture for 4 minutes on high pressure. Remove from the heat. Let the pressure release naturally.

Makes 6 to 8 servings
11 minutes at low pressure

black forest **croissant** pudding

Bread pudding is an indulgent dessert, but pudding made with buttery croissants is downright decadent. With chocolate and dried cherries, it becomes even more sinful. Like the bread for bread pudding, the croissants should be dry and firm to soak up the custard. To dry soft, fresh croissants, bake in a preheated 300°F oven for 10 to 12 minutes, then cool completely. This pudding is best served warm, as the butter in the croissants gets hard when refrigerated.

2 cups milk
⅓ cup packed light brown sugar
6 ounces high-quality bittersweet or semisweet
   chocolate, finely chopped
4 large eggs, at room temperature, well-beaten
1 teaspoon vanilla
4 day-old croissants, torn into bite-sized pieces
   (3½ packed cups)
⅔ cup dried cherries
Butter, for the soufflé dish and foil
Sweetened whipped cream, for serving

1. Lightly butter a 1½-quart soufflé dish and set aside.

2. In a medium saucepan over medium heat, cook the milk and brown sugar, stirring often to dissolve the sugar, until small bubbles appear around the edges of the milk.

3. Place the chocolate in a large bowl. Pour the hot milk mixture over the chocolate and let stand for 3 minutes. Whisk until the mixture is smooth. Gradually whisk the beaten eggs into the chocolate mixture. Whisk in the vanilla. Stir in the croissants and dried cherries. Let stand for 10 minutes, stirring occasionally.

4. Place the trivet into a 5- to 7-quart pressure cooker. Pour 2 cups of water into the cooker.

5. Pour the croissant mixture into the prepared dish. Butter the center of a piece of aluminum foil, and tightly cover the dish, centering the buttered area over the pudding. Using an aluminum foil "cradle" (see page 145), lower the dish into the cooker. Lock the lid in place. Bring to high pressure over high heat. Adjust the heat to maintain the pressure. Cook for 25 minutes. Remove from the heat and quick-release the pressure.

6. Open the lid, tilting it away from you to block any escaping steam. Using the cradle, remove the pudding. Remove the foil. The pudding should feel barely set when pressed in the center—it will firm upon standing. If necessary, re-cover the pudding with foil, return to the cooker, and pressure-cook on high for an additional 2 minutes. Cool the pudding for 10 minutes. Serve warm, with the whipped cream.

_____

Makes 6 servings
25 minutes at high pressure

cranberry **bread** pudding

A s a warm winter dessert, this cranberry bread pudding is hard to beat. Be sure to use day-old bread, or dry it in a 300°F oven for 10 to 12 minutes. Serve the pudding with a drizzle of heavy cream.

4 large eggs plus 1 large egg yolk
⅔ cup sugar
4 tablespoons unsalted butter, melted
1⅔ cups half-and-half
Grated zest of 1 orange
½ teaspoon vanilla extract
5 cups (½-inch cubes) packed day-old firm white sandwich bread
½ cup dried cranberries
Butter, for the soufflé dish and foil
½ cup heavy cream, for serving

1. In a large bowl, whisk the eggs, yolk, and sugar until well combined. Gradually whisk in the melted butter. Whisk in the half-and-half, orange zest, and vanilla. Add the bread cubes and cranberries and mix well. Let stand for 10 to 15 minutes so the bread can soak up the custard.

2. Place the trivet into a 5- to 7-quart pressure cooker. Pour 2 cups of water into the cooker. Lightly butter a 1½-quart soufflé dish.

3. Pour the bread mixture into the dish. Butter the center of a piece of aluminum foil, and tightly cover the dish, centering the buttered area over the pudding. Using an aluminum foil "cradle" (see page 145), lower the dish into the cooker. Lock the lid in place. Bring to high pressure over high heat. Adjust the heat to maintain the pressure. Cook for 16 minutes. Remove from the heat and quick-release the pressure.

4. Open the lid, tilting it away from you to block any escaping steam. Using the cradle, remove the pudding. Remove the foil. The pudding should feel barely set when pressed in the center—it will firm upon standing. If necessary, re-cover the pudding with foil, return to the cooker, and pressure-cook on high for an additional 2 minutes. Cool the pudding for 10 minutes. Serve warm, pouring a bit of cream over each serving.

⸻

Makes 4 to 6 servings
16 minutes at high pressure

"no-cook" orchard applesauce

Applesauce is a comforting snack. We call this "no cook" because all you do is bring the apples to high pressure in the cooker, then turn it off immediately. You can use any apple you like (just not Red Delicious, which are best for eating and make a mealy sauce), but the recipe is probably best with a combination. For example, sweet Golden Delicious apples match well with tart Pippins or Empires. Or try juicy Jonathan apples with sweet MacIntosh. The final flavor varies according to the apples used, so be flexible—you may have to simmer the sauce a few minutes to reduce excess liquid and intensify the apple flavor (there goes the "no cook" theory!).

6 medium (2½ pounds total) apples, peeled, cored, and cut into ¼-inch-thick wedges
½ cup water
½ cup sugar
1 cinnamon stick or ⅛ teaspoon ground cinnamon
One 4-inch strip lemon zest, removed from the lemon with a vegetable peeler

1. In a 5- to 7-quart pressure cooker, combine the apples, water, sugar, cinnamon stick, and lemon zest. Lock the lid in place. Bring to high pressure over high heat. Immediately remove from the heat and quick-release the pressure. Open the lid, tilting it away from you to block any escaping steam. Discard the cinnamon stick and lemon zest. Stir well to break up the apples. If desired, return the pot, uncovered, to high heat and bring to a boil. Cook, stirring often, until the applesauce has thickened to the desired consistency. Serve warm. Or cool to room temperature, cover, and refrigerate until chilled, about 2 hours.

Savory Rosemary Applesauce: This is an excellent condiment for roast pork. Stir 1 teaspoon Demi-Glace Rapide (page 27) and 1 teaspoon chopped fresh rosemary into the applesauce. Serve chilled.

———

Makes about 2½ cups
Bring to high pressure, then quick-release

riesling pears with mascarpone and almonds

I f you are looking for a delicious, easy dessert with only a few well-chosen ingredients, this is it. Add speedy preparation to these qualities, and the result is a dessert you'll return to again and again, especially for dinner parties where you need to present something elegant with a minimum of fuss. The better the wine, the better the results. Use 1 cup to cook the pears, then chill and serve the remainder in small glasses with the dessert.

⅓ cup sliced almonds
4 medium firm-ripe Bosc pears
1 lemon, cut in half
1 cup fruity semi-dry white wine, such as
    Johannesburg Riesling
¼ cup sugar
6 ounces mascarpone cheese, at room temperature
Mint sprigs, for garnish

1. Position a rack in the center of the oven and preheat to 350°F. Spread the almonds on a baking sheet. Bake, stirring occasionally, until the almonds are toasted, about 10 minutes. Transfer the almonds to a plate and cool completely. Set aside.

2. Peel the pears and cut in half lengthwise. Using a melon baller, remove the tough core from each pear half. Rub the pears with the lemon halves to prevent discoloring.

3. In a 5- to 7-quart pressure cooker, combine the wine and sugar. Arrange the pears in the cooker and spoon the wine over them. Lock the lid in place. Bring to high pressure over high heat. Adjust the heat to maintain the pressure. Cook for 1 minute. Remove from the heat and quick-release the pressure.

Open the lid, tilting it away from you to block any escaping steam. Using a slotted spoon, transfer to a deep platter. Pour the wine syrup over the pears and cool completely. Cover with plastic wrap and refrigerate until chilled, at least 1 hour or overnight.

4. To serve, place two pear halves, cut sides up, in a shallow bowl. Fill the hollow of each pear with a dollop of mascarpone and sprinkle with almonds. Drizzle with some of the wine syrup and garnish with the mint. Repeat with the remaining ingredients. Serve chilled.

Makes 4 servings
1 minute at high pressure

dried fruit **compote** with merlot and spices

One of the quickest desserts on the planet, this is especially welcome during winter months when the selection of seasonal fresh fruits is limited. If you don't care to use whole cinnamon and cloves, substitute ¼ teaspoon ground cinnamon and a pinch of ground cloves. Serve the chilled compote over vanilla ice cream or orange sorbet, or by itself with crisp cookies. It does double-duty as a fine accompaniment to grilled pork chops or roast pork loin.

1 large orange
1 cinnamon stick
5 whole cloves
8 ounces dried apricots, cut in half lengthwise
4 ounces (1 cup) dried cranberries
½ cup raisins
½ cup fruity red wine, such as Merlot
⅓ cup packed light brown sugar
2 Granny Smith or Rome apples or Bosc pears,
   each peeled, cored, and cut lengthwise into
   8 wedges
2 tablespoons dark rum

1. Grate the zest from the orange. Squeeze the juice from the orange into a measuring cup, and add enough water to measure ½ cup. Wrap the cinnamon and cloves in a rinsed piece of cheesecloth and tie into a sachet.

2. Place the dried apricots, dried cranberries, raisins, wine, orange juice mixture, brown sugar, and orange zest in a 5- to 7-quart pressure cooker, and bury the spice sachet in the mixture. Place the apple wedges on top.

3. Lock the lid in place. Bring to high pressure over high heat. Adjust the heat to maintain the pressure. Cook for 1 minute. Remove from the heat and quick-release the pressure. Open the lid, tilting it away from you to block any escaping steam. Using a slotted spoon, transfer the fruit to a medium bowl. Remove the cinnamon stick.

4. Return the uncovered pot to high heat and bring the cooking liquid to a boil. Boil until thickened and evaporated by about half, about 5 minutes. Stir in the rum. Pour over the fruit and cool to room temperature. Cover tightly and refrigerate until chilled, at least 2 hours.

Makes 4 servings
1 minute at high pressure

pear-cranberry chutney

Most pressure cooker manufacturers warn against making cranberry sauce in the cooker, as the berries foam up during cooking and the tiny seeds could block a vent. However, with precautions, you can make some cranberry sauces. We place sliced pears (you can also use Granny Smith apples) on top of the cranberry mixture to discourage any foaming. This zesty recipe makes a crowd-sized batch to serve with the holiday turkey or crown roast of pork. Don't make it in an unlined aluminum cooker.

One 12-ounce bag cranberries, rinsed and picked over
1 cup packed light brown sugar
1 small onion, finely chopped
1 jalapeño pepper, seeded and minced
2 tablespoons shredded fresh ginger (use the large holes on a box grater)
1 garlic clove, finely chopped
1 teaspoon yellow mustard seed
One 3-inch cinnamon stick
¼ teaspoon salt
3 pounds ripe Bartlett pears, peeled, cored, and cut lengthwise into 1-inch-wide wedges

1. In a 5- to 7-quart pressure cooker, combine the cranberries, brown sugar, onion, jalapeño, ginger, garlic, mustard, cinnamon stick, and salt. Cook over medium heat, uncovered, stirring often, until the sugar dissolves. Place the pears over the cranberry mixture.

2. Lock the lid in place. Bring to high pressure over high heat. Adjust the heat to maintain the pressure. Cook for 1 minute. Remove from the heat and quick-release the pressure. Open the lid, tilting it away from you to block any escaping steam. Remove the cinnamon stick. Cool completely. (The chutney can be prepared up to 2 weeks ahead, covered tightly in an airtight container, and refrigerated.)

Makes about 1½ quarts, 12 to 16 servings
1 minute at high pressure

index

index

table of equivalents

The exact equivalents in the following tables have been rounded for convenience.

LIQUID/DRY MEASURES

U.S.	METRIC
¼ teaspoon	1.25 milliliters
½ teaspoon	2.5 milliliters
1 teaspoon	5 milliliters
1 tablespoon (3 teaspoons)	15 milliliters
1 fluid ounce (2 tablespoons)	30 milliliters
¼ cup	60 milliliters
⅓ cup	80 milliliters
½ cup	120 milliliters
1 cup	240 milliliters
1 pint (2 cups)	480 milliliters
1 quart (4 cups, 32 ounces)	960 milliliters
1 gallon (4 quarts)	3.84 liters
1 ounce (by weight)	28 grams
1 pound	454 grams
2.2 pounds	1 kilogram

OVEN TEMPERATURE

FAHRENHEIT	CELSIUS	GAS
250	120	½
275	140	1
300	150	2
325	160	3
350	180	4
375	190	5
400	200	6
425	220	7
450	230	8
475	240	9
500	260	10

LENGTH

U.S.	METRIC
⅛ inch	3 millimeters
¼ inch	6 millimeters
½ inch	12 millimeters
1 inch	2.5 centimeters